Gay Life
in Dutch Society

Gay Life
in Dutch Society

Edited by
A. X. van Naerssen

Gay Life in Dutch Society was simultaneously issued by The Haworth Press, Inc., under the title: *Interdisciplinary Research on Homosexuality in the Netherlands* and simultaneously published as a special issue of the *Journal of Homosexuality*, Volume 13, Numbers 2/3, Winter 1986/Spring 1987, A. X. van Naerssen, Guest Editor.

Harrington Park Press
New York • London

Published by

Harrington Park Press, Inc., 12 West 32 Street, New York, New York 10001
EUROSPAN/Harrington, 3 Henrietta Street, London WC2E 8LU England

Harrington Park Press, Inc., is a subsidiary of The Haworth Press, Inc., 12 West 32 Street, New York, New York 10001.

Gay Life in Dutch Society was originally published as *Journal of Homosexuality*, Volume 13, Numbers 2/3, Winter 1986/Spring 1987.

Cover design by Marshall Andrews.

Library of Congress Cataloging-in-Publication Data

Interdisciplinary research on homosexuality in the Netherlands.
    Gay life in Dutch society.

    Originally published as: Interdisciplinary research on homosexuality in the Netherlands.
    1. Homosexuality—Netherlands. 2. Homosexuals—Netherlands. 3. Social work with homosexuals—Netherlands. I. Naerssen, A. X. van. II. Title.
HQ76.3.N4I58   1987a   306.7'66'09492   87-391
ISBN 0-918393-39-6

CONTENTS

Gay Life
in Dutch Society

Preface

These two issues of the *Journal of Homosexuality* continue our effort to publish research that is international in scope, in this case by scholars in The Netherlands. There are several reasons why the *Journal* has sought to do this. First of all, much provocative research is occurring elsewhere and generally unknown by Americans or inaccessible because it exists in foreign languages. Research on homosexuality has gathered impressive momentum particularly in The Netherlands, partly because of the warm reception it enjoys in several Dutch universities. Second, the European tradition of research in the social sciences is quite different from that in the United States. Whereas in the United States it tends to be empirical and atheoretical, in Europe authors are more explicit about their theoretical and ideological commitments and often use evidence from several disciplines to illuminate their inquiry into homosexuality. European scholarship, therefore, is not self-consciously "interdisciplinary" since it does not occur to authors there to halt their inquiry into homosexuality at the boundaries of any one discipline. Third, with an international perspective on homosexuality, each nation can identify what is idiosyncratic or general—that which seems to be a product of local circumstances and history and that which reflects the broader beliefs, social attitudes, and political and moral structures of western civilization.

I want to express my deepest appreciation to Professor Lex van Naerssen of the State University of Utrecht for bravely and successfully coordinating this effort of bringing Dutch research on homosexuality to readers of the *Journal*. It involved his working with peripatetic scholars whose home bases are at several universities in The Netherlands and with the vicissitudes of transoceanic mail. I also thank him and the authors for their

ix

almost Job-like patience in getting this project underway, the cordiality they afforded me at Utrecht when we met to ceremonialize its start, and their generous response to the requests of the indefatigable manuscript editor, Norman Hopper. I thank Corlynn Cognata for preparing several of the abstracts and her faithful assistance to Mr. Hopper and, my secretary, Donna Munoz.

John P. De Cecco, Editor
San Francisco

Gay Life
in Dutch Society

Edited by
A. X. van Naerssen

Gay Life in Dutch Society was simultaneously issued by The Haworth Press, Inc., under the title: *Interdisciplinary Research on Homosexuality in the Netherlands* and simultaneously published as a special issue of the *Journal of Homosexuality*, Volume 13, Numbers 2/3, Winter 1986/Spring 1987, A. X. van Naerssen, Guest Editor.

Harrington Park Press
New York • London

A Research Into Homosexuality
in The Netherlands

A. X. van Naerssen

University of Utrecht

ABSTRACT. This article presents varying ideologies regarding homosexuality. The history of homosexual research is reviewed from a clinical and sociological perspective. Centers for research in the area of homosexuality in The Netherlands are described in terms of their area of study as well as their differing ideological views. In conclusion, the increased awareness of the Dutch Government and the governance of the Dutch universities of the importance of research into homosexuality is described.

CLINICAL STUDIES

Up to the mid-1960s, the research into homosexuality remained limited to a number of clinical psychiatric studies. Homosexuality was looked upon as a psychic disposition which probably originated from early youth. Coen van Emde Boas (1965), a prominent sexologist-psychiatrist, departed from the orthodox psychoanalytical theory and assumed that the male homosexual orientation developed from a fear of castration combined with an over-strong identification with the mother. At the same time he recognized that the phenomenon of exclusive homosexuality remained unresolved by psychoanalytic theory. In 1967 C. van den Aardweg, a psychologist, published a study entitled "Homophilia, Neurosis and Compulsive Self-Pity." He.

The guest editor of these issues, Lex van Naerssen, is a member of the Interfacultary Group of Lesbian/Gay Studies at the State University of Utrecht and Acting Chair of the Clinical Sexology Department. Correspondence may be addressed to the author, Vakgroep Klinische Psychologie, Postbus 80140, 3508 TC Utrecht, The Netherlands.

1

defended the thesis that homosexual desires were to be regarded as infantile feelings resulting from a youth's rejection by his peers. In contrast to the psychoanalysts, he presupposed that homosexuality could be disposed of once those concerned had gained insight into their own psycho-sexual development. He described some of his therapies in his book, therapies which gave rise to heated controversies. Although the gay-emancipation movement repudiated his points of departure, and professionals considered his research method vague and unsystematic, his hypothesis that homosexuals were predominantly more neurotic than heterosexuals was maintained. It was not until 1974 that Geert Sanders, in a survey of American studies, showed that no empirical support could be found for the notion of a homosexual neurosis. In recent years, the Dutch Federation of Psychologists, in which van den Aardweg used to hold an important position, has been taking reserved stands. Their official point of view, which was formulated in 1980, was that homosexual desires could be changed through psychotherapy, and that attempts to that effect should be undertaken if a client wishes to. (For a more detailed description of this situation see van Naerssen's article in this issue.)

FROM CLINICAL TO SOCIO-PSYCHOLOGICAL STUDIES (1976-1977)

In 1969 the socio-psychiatrist Wijnand Sengers published his thesis "Homosexuality as a Complaint." He suggested labeling someone a male homosexual only if certain criteria were met: A person had to feel exclusively attracted to persons of his sex, and during masturbation his dreams and sexual fantasies should exclusively relate to those of his own sex. Senger's system became generally accepted by Dutch psychiatrists and subsequently served as a directive in diagnosing homosexuality.

According to Sengers, it was practically senseless to strive to change homosexuals, for apart from their sexual preference, homosexuals are identical to heterosexuals. If homosexuals needed therapy, it should focus on fostering their self-acceptance, for their fears, uncertainties, and depressions often resulted from their denying their homosexuality.

Sengers' theory also had a great influence on counseling (cf. van Naerssen's article), and his views were also adopted in a number of socio-psychological studies (Moerings & Straver, 1970; Sanders, 1977). In these studies the phases of the self-acceptance process and the factors that positively influenced this process, i.e., led to self-acceptance, were investigated. In Sanders' research approximately 500 young homosexuals were examined. He showed that acceptance of someone's sexual preference by parents, friends, and contemporaries enhanced the chances of a positive self-acceptance. Grubb (1983) pointed out in his study of gay reading (cf. his article in this issue) relevant differences between these Dutch identity studies and similar studies in the United States. He labeled the American studies of homosexual development linear-progressive, and the Dutch open-ended: "In the linear-progressive model, attention seems to be paid more to the affirmative action involved in the perception of one's homosexual options. One is working towards being an up-front gay person. It might not be too broad an interpretation to say that, in terms of this model, what one is working toward is a selfhood in which sexuality, positively manifested, acts as a major identifying device."

In contrast, the open-ended model applied in the Dutch studies described how people are taught to look upon their homosexuality as something not fundamentally different from heterosexuality. The goal of the homosexual development was a complete psychological and social integration.

SOCIOLOGICAL STUDIES OF HOMOSEXUALITY

Straver (1976) published a survey of the sociological studies that were undertaken during the period 1965 to 1975, studies in which the following problems were examined: the views on homosexuality and homosexual men and women in (1) a representative random sample of the Dutch people; (2) a representative random sample of people concerned with information, education, and counseling in the field of homosexuality; and (3) a similar sample of people involved in appointing homosexuals in various work situations (Meilof-Oonk, 1969; Meilof-Oonk, Valkman, 1973; De Boer e.a., 1974). These studies revealed that the notion that homosexuality was as "normal" as heterosexuality still met with much social resistance, and provided the gay-emancipation movement with starting points for the development of social policy which would integrate homosexuality in society.

In his work "Homosexuality in The Netherlands," a study of an emancipation movement, (Tielman, 1982) Tielman described how this integration largely succeeded, analyzing the development of the emancipation of homosexuality from 1911 to the present. The integration of homosexuals into Dutch society has been facilitated by the fact that Dutch Society is subdivided into a relatively large number of political and religious groups, divisions, which can be encountered in all fields of public life. For example, in 1982, 80 percent of the population was tolerant of homosexuality, and 42 percent thought that homosexuality was normal (Hoogma, 1984).

THE SITUATION BETWEEN 1979 AND 1984

Tielman's study indicated how, in scientific reasoning, attention began shifting from homosexuality as a sexual deviation to homosexuality as an expression of sexuality which, to a greater or lesser extent, has socially discriminating consequences. Over the same period, various groups in The Netherlands ventured to change how other ways of sexual expression, i.e., partner exchange, open marriage, pederasty, and sado-masochism were viewed, but no group was influential enough to draw any other sexual lifestyle out of the province of medico-psychological pathology.

Since 1977, centers for the study of homosexuality have been set up at various Dutch universities, the majority started at the initiative of teachers and students working within the social science faculties that in The Netherlands are subdivided into the following departments: psychology, education, sociology, and cultural anthropology. However, it has been difficult to give these centers a formal position within the university structure.

The center of gay studies in Utrecht has been the most successful thus far, and is manned by part-time assistants who work with the psychology, sociology, languages, history, law, and medicine departments. Having chosen homosexuality and emancipation for a theme, these assistants spend a great deal of time lecturing on the subject of gay studies. As to the research program, the lecturers and students are entirely dependent on grants. The program focuses on the causes and effects of social discrimination on homosexual relationships, with the aim of developing strategies for countering this discrimination. The range of subjects the program deals with is wide, including:

Socio-Historical: The ways of life and emancipation of lesbians in The Netherlands (Schreurs, 1985). The suppression of homosexuality in The Netherlands during World War II (Koenders, 1984).

Sociological: Discrimination against homosexuality by social institutions (e.g., through legal regulations, at schools) and its influence on the day-to-day life of homosexuals (Hoogma, 1984).

Psychological: Inquiries into the relationships between gay men and lesbians, and into the counseling of homosexual clients (van Naerssen, 1985).

Juridical: The contemplated anti-discrimination legislation

and its relation to discrimination on the ground of sexual preference (Waaldijk and Tielman, 1984).

Socio-Medical: A socio-scientific examination of people be-
longing to the AIDS high-risk group (see Tielman, this issue).

AMSTERDAM

The center in Amsterdam is part of the Department of "Ver-
zorgingssociologie" and formally has a smaller base of support
than the center in Utrecht. Over the past few years it has successfully organized seminars which dealt with the theme of the
sociological and historical recognition of homosocial arrangements. This theme was also discussed at the conference "Among
men, among women" (Amsterdam, June, 1983), which was attended by 200 participants. About 80 papers were presented at
that occasion on a variety of homosocial phenomena. Especially
the views on homosexuality as defended by Foucault (1976),
Weeks (1977), and Plummer (1981), had a prominent place in
the methodological approach of most studies. The research team
of Amsterdam avoids the term homosexuality, as they think it
does not define the field they feel they ought to study. They re-
ject the approach advocated by Utrecht because they feel that
approach too much emphasizes the contrast between homosexuality and heterosexuality and remains coupled to the medico-
clinical notion of homosexuality as a disease, a sexual deviation,
or a deviant social lifestyle. The Amsterdam team believes that
the homosexual way of life is but one of the many examples of
homosexual contact. Their intention is to focus on all aspects of
a relationship between persons of the same sex (homo-social arrangements), and to pay more attention to history, especially the
19th and 20th centuries. Thus, for instance, they have attempted
to analyze how the medical views of homosexuality have influenced the views of other forms of homosexual conduct
(Sociologische Gids, 1985).

SOCIAL SCIENTIFIC RESEARCH ON AIDS

The problem of the AIDS epidemic makes it clear that both points of view are useful in analyzing, in a country with a certain tolerance to different sexual lifestyles, reactions to the threats of a severe disease. One sees in the social scientific research on AIDS studies on the social discrimination of persons labeled as homosexual and on the construction of homosexuality in different subcultures (Sociologische Gids, 1985). So the more pragmatic view on discrimination of homosexuality, as defended by gay studies at Utrecht, and the definition of homosexuality as a construction influenced by a multitude of social and historical influences, do not exclude each other.

More important than ideological differences is the fact that the Dutch Government and the Boards of the Universities gradually recognize that gay studies, defined as an interdisciplinary approach on homosexuality, are fruitful and necessary.

REFERENCES

Aardweg, G. J. A. van den (1967). *Homofilie, neurose en dwangzelfbeklag*. Amsterdam: Polak en van Gennep.
Boer, J. de e. a. (1974). *Meningen over homosexualiteit III*. Een onderzoek naar problemen voor homosexuelen in de beroepssituatie. Den Haag: Staatsuitgeverij.
Emde, Boas C. van (1965). Enkele aspecten van het probleem van de mannelijke homosexualiteit. *Huisarts en Wetenschap*.
Foucault, M. (1976). *La volonté de savoir, histoire de la sexualité*. Paris: Editions Gallimard.
Grubb, P. F. (1983). *You got it from all those books*. A study of gay reading. Unpublished doctoral thesis, University of Amsterdam.
Homostudies, Sociologie en Seksualiteit (1985). Special issue of "*Sociologische Gids*," Sociological Guide.
Hoogma, M. (1984). *Wet en Werkelijkheid*. Homostudies, Utrecht.
Koenders, P. (1984). *Homoseksualiteit in bezet Nederland*. Amsterdam: SUA.
Meilof-Oonk, (1969). *Meningen over homosexualiteit II*. Amsterdam: Stichting ter bevordering Sociaal Onderzoek Minderheden.
Meilof-Oonk, S., & Valkman, O. (1973). *Meningen over homosexualiteit II*. Amsterdam: Stichting ter bevordering Sociaal Onderzoek Minderheden.
Moerings, M., & Straver, C. (1970). *Homofiele jongeren in relatie tot hun omgeving*. Zeist.

Naerssen, A. X. van (1985). *Homoseksualiteit: Geaardheid, verlangen, identiteit of rol.* Homojaarboek, 3. Amsterdam: van Gennep.

Plummer, K. (Ed.) (1981). The making of the modern homosexual. London: Hutchinson.

Sanders, G. (1974). *Homosexualiteit. Een overzicht van het sociaal- weten- schappelijk onderzoek naar homosexualiteit in Amerika en West-Europa.* Zeist: Nisso.

Sanders, G. (1977). *Het genone en het byzonde van de homoseksuele leefsituatie,* Deventer, Van Loghum Slaterus.

Schreurs, K. (1985). *Het is maar hoe je het bekijkt.* Homostudies, Utrecht.

Straver, C. J. (1976). Research on homosexuality in the Netherlands. *The Netherlands Journal of Sociology, 12,* 121-137.

Tielman, R. (1982). *Homoseksualiteit in Nederland,* Boom, Meppel.

Waaldijk, C., & Tielman, R. (1984). *Grondrechtenafweging en de Wet Gelijke Behandeling.* Homostudies, Utrecht.

Weeks, J. (1977). Coming out: Homosexual politics in Britain from the Nineteenth Century to the present. London: Quartet Books.

Dutch Gay Emancipation History (1911-1986)

Rob Tielman
University of Utrecht

ABSTRACT. The Dutch homosexual movement is one of the oldest and most influential in the world.[1] The aim of this article is to describe how this success can be explained both by some specific characteristics of Dutch society and ideologies, strategies, and tactics as developed by the gay movement. Although it is always risky to make a comparison with other countries and the homosexual movements there, I try to point out briefly some distinct differences and similarities.

A HISTORICAL OVERVIEW

Prior to 1911

As in the rest of Western Europe, the Dutch Middle Ages were characterized by a prevailing anti-homosexual climate.[2] As far as we know there was no room for overt homosexuality. There are some indications that informal networks of "sodomites" came into being in the larger cities, but the members of such networks led an underground existence. In 1730, during a period of instability, mainly due to an economical and political decline in The Netherlands, hundreds of sodomites were persecuted as scapegoats.[3]

Under the influence of the French Revolution, the law penal-

Dr. Tielman is a sociologist and Head of the Gay Studies Department of the University of Utrecht, Heidelberglaan 1, 3584 CS, Utrecht, The Netherlands. The author wishes to thank Walter Huyten and Judith Schuyf for the translation of this article, and Lex Van Naerssen and Tom Verdijk for their helpful comments. Correspondence may be sent to the author at the above address.

izing sodomy was abolished in 1811, a result not so much of a changed view on homosexuality as of an altered view of the role of the state.[4] One of the consequences of the separation of church and state was the abolishment of criminal persecution of sexual acts between mutually consenting adults.[5] This rather liberal legislation was brought to an end in 1911 when a coalition of Christian parties restored the state to its moralist position. However, the Christian reaction to the neutral liberal state did not mean a total return to the situation preceding the French Revolution, when the Dutch (Calvinist) state church played a dominant role. The establishment of a Christian political majority had been accomplished primarily by the cooperation of two religious minority groups, the Roman Catholics and Calvinists. Their aim was not so much the reinstatement of the old state church as it was a state-subsidized autonomy for their own communities and provisions.

Thus came into being the typical Dutch phenomenon called "pillarization" (verzuiling),[6] i.e., the splitting up of society into socially separated denominational sectors, each taking care of his own social, state-subventioned provisions (education, mass media, hospitals, housing, and so forth). This pillarization profoundly affected Dutch society in such a way that socio-political majorities could subsequently exist only through coalitions of minorities, all of which wanted to be as autonomous as possible. The "pillars" used state power and finance to weaken state influence on the denominational freedom of the four (Calvinist, Roman Catholic, socialist, and liberal) minorities.

1911 to 1940

In 1911 the re-introduction of legal discrimination of homosexuals by the Christian political coalition brought forth the possibility of penalizing homosexual contacts between adults and minors. In reaction, the liberal jurist Jacob Schorer founded the Dutch Scientific Humanitarian Committee (Nederlandsch Wetenschappelijk Humanitair Komitee: NWHK)[7] based on Magnus Hirschfeld's German WHK of 1898.[8]

The NWHK sought to accomplish political and social equality for homosexual men and women by counteracting prejudiced information on this subject. The NWHK was fiercely opposed by Roman Catholics, Calvinists, and, later, also by Dutch Nazis,[9] and it could only count on limited support from liberal and socialist groups. Characteristic for the NWHK was the "key-figure" strategy, whereby it approached influential persons to enlighten them on the subject of homosexuality. The NWHK avoided an open confrontation with Dutch society and the development of a gay subculture as much as possible for fear, in those days not without reason, that such a strategy might work out in a contrary manner.

Just before World War II, an independent group of homosexuals, connected with the periodical *Levensrecht* (Right to Live), wanted to emphasize forming a gay subculture more than trying to change the mentality of key figures, as done by the NWHK. Yet they were no less overtaken by the German invasion of May 10, 1940 than was the rest of Dutch society.

1940 to 1945

The German occupation forces dissolved the NWHK and, on July 30, 1940, proclaimed all sexual conduct between men illegal. Although the Germans made an attempt systematically to persecute homosexual men, they were not successful in doing so on a large scale.[11]

Contrary to Germany, homosexual acts between consenting adults had not been punishable in The Netherlands prior to the occupation; therefore, the introduction of punishment for homosexuals did not appeal to the Dutch sense of justice. Second, the Dutch homosexual subculture had remained underground all the time, in contrast to that in Berlin in the 1920s, and was therefore less susceptible to persecution. Third, the Dutch police were unwilling to cooperate in the persecution. As far as can be ascertained, the registration lists of homosexuals were not handed over to the Germans. After World War II this persecution remained for decades a concealed chapter in historical publications.

1946 to 1964

In 1946, the editors of Levensrecht, who had been in hiding during the war, became the founding members of the Cultural and Recreational Centre (Cultuur- en OntspanningsCentrum COC), the successor of the NWHK. First and foremost, the COC functioned as a refuge for homosexual men and women amidst social oppression.[12] Apart from that, the old strategy of the NWHK was maintained, that of fostering social acceptance through information and contact with key social figures.

The main opposition to the COC was led by Roman Catholics, who tried to induce the government to bar it and to outlaw homosexual acts between consenting adults. But the COC was tolerated by Dutch authorities, for the existence of that group enabled them to keep a better eye on the homosexual subculture. In fact, the government treated the COC more and more as a "mini-pillar": The COC had a certain autonomy that enabled it to maintain order in the gay subculture. The leader of this minipillar were constantly in informal and covert contact with some key figures within the real pillars: the Roman Catholics, the Protestants, the socialists, and the liberals. These key figures had a relatively more positive attitude toward homosexuality as a result of their professional background and their social minority position, which forced them to communicate with people of other pillars. Gradually, changes in mentality, slowly achieved at the top, were conveyed to important parts of the leaders' constituencies.

In addition, the COC tried to develop an international strategy by founding the International Committee for Sexual Equality in

1951. Participating in the ICSE were homosexual organizations from countries including Switzerland, France, Germany, Denmark, Norway, Sweden, Great Britain, and the United States. However, the ICSE was maintained by the COC (it being the largest homosexual organization in the world at that time) and died a silent death in 1960 when it became clear that the other homosexual organizations were too weak to maintain an international organization.

1964 to 1971

The changing social climate of the 1960s led the COC to be more open.[13] In 1964 a foundation was set up to promote a dialogue with Dutch society. Taking advantage of the change of mentality that had taken place in the meantime, the COC reached an ever-growing part of Dutch society by propagating the insight that "homophiles," as was the popular euphemism for homosexuals at the time, were "just the same." Twice, however, the COC was denied incorporation by the government, which was still dominated by Christian political parties, because the government refused to accept homosexuals as equals by giving the COC legal status. The key-figure strategy did succeed in bringing an end to the penalization of homosexual contacts between adults and minors, which took place in 1971, after it was generally accepted that homosexual "seduction" was not possible after the age of 6.

Late in the 1960s it proved possible to begin setting up large-scale social research on the origin and occurrence of discrimination against homosexuals.[14] During the 1970s such research helped foster a government policy against the discrimination of homosexuals. Also during the late 1960s an influential homosexual student movement came into being which succeeded in 1971 in changing the COC ideology of assimilation of homosexuals into a more radical ideology of the integration of homosexuality by changing the heterosexual character of society. Since that time, homosexual students and intellectuals have played a more important role in the Dutch gay movement.

1971 to 1986

Several factors led to a more favorable climate for the Dutch gay movement in the 1970s: the increasing openness about sexuality in general and homosexuality in specific; the social disengagement of sexuality from procreation, marriage, and gender roles; the growing influence of the women's liberation movement; and finally, the fact that, due to the strongly increased secularization of society, Christian political power diminished in favor of liberal/socialist political power.[15]

The COC was given legal status by the government in 1973 and got subvention for its activities from that moment on. Various forms of discrimination were abolished by the government, constitutional equality was achieved in 1983, and an anti-discrimination law including homosexuals came under consideration.[16] At this writing, a vast majority, 86% of Dutch society is of the opinion that homosexuals are to be treated with equality, as opposed to 56% who were of that opinion in 1968. In 1968, 60% of the Dutch gave opinions about homosexuality as being dirty, deviant, or abnormal; in 1981, fewer than 10% did.[17]

INTERNATIONAL COMPARISON

The key strategy has now changed into a more overt variant: The so-called gay caucus strategy. Within political parties, trade-unions, educational institutions, churches, mass media, and so on, homosexual working groups are formed to secure the interests of fellow homosexuals. In this manner many alliances are being made in Dutch society, including ones with influential women's liberation caucuses, which are of great strategical importance. Partly because of the discriminating legislation from

1911 to 1971, which affected both homosexual men and homosexual women, a close cooperation has always existed between these groups in the Dutch gay movement; this in turn has fostered the alliance between the gay and women's liberation movements. During the 1970s two other strategies for homosexual women were developed outside the gay movement: lesbian groups within women's liberation, and later autonomous lesbian groups.[18] Participation of homosexual women in the gay movement has increased considerably since 1970 (from 15% to 40%).

Since the mid-1970s the debate on the COC's ideology and strategy has been reopened, especially by relatively small groups of radical lesbians and gay men. A certain separation is their aim, whereas the COC still has as its goal integration, regarded not as assimilation but as the development of a proper, non-isolated identity, of participation in society on an equal footing. This integration model can be seen as a modern version of the traditional Dutch pillarization. A number of differences between the homosexual population in The Netherlands and those in other countries can be observed. In other parts of the world, gay ghettos have come into existence in some big cities. In The Netherlands homosexuals live all over the country with their own geographically spread provisions. And the influence of the COC on those provisions is relatively larger than that of "gay capitalism," which often has a common interest with anti-homosexual circles in isolating homosexuals from the rest of society by making them dependent of those groups' business.

As a result of the gay student movement of the late 1960s, homosexuals became influential in determining the direction of social research related to homosexuality. Whereas in other countries considerable attention is paid to subcultural lifestyles, most Dutch researchers of homosexuality focus on the causes of, and possible ways to change, discrimination against homosexuals in society. Research has focused on discrimination in counseling, education, employment, housing, mass media, police, political parties, medical care, legal practice, and science itself. These

studies help support the effectiveness of the Dutch gay movement in attaining equal rights for homosexuals in daily life. At
the Utrecht University an official Gay Studies Department has
been established for this kind of research.

The effectiveness of the different ideologies, strategies, and
the tactics utilized by the Dutch gay movement can be evaluated
in the 1980s by observing the reactions of different societies and
gay movements to Acquired Immunity Deficiency Syndrome
(AIDS). At first glance, neither assimilation nor segregation
seem to have led to an adequate social response to AIDS. This
disease has often been used as a means to discredit homosexuals.
The interests of homosexuals could only be safeguarded in those
countries, e.g., The Netherlands, where the gay movement had
had the opportunity to develop its own identity, and was thus
able to act as a collective entity in attempting to gain social recognition and rights, establishing itself in the mainstream of society by alliances with other minority groups. This alliances strategy protected the Dutch gay minority against scapegoating
processes because of AIDS and enabled it to influence the AIDS
policy of Dutch government.[19] The effectiveness of the Dutch
gay emancipation movement cannot be seen apart from specific
characteristics of Dutch society and history. Nevertheless it is
worthwhile for other gay emancipation movements elsewhere to
analyze the usefulness of strategies of integration or alliance.
Unfortunately such an international comparison cannot now be
made because of a lacking development of gay studies in other
parts of the world.

NOTES

1. This article is a brief summary of my thesis: *Homosexualiteit in Nederland,
studie van een emancipatiebeweging* (Homosexuality in The Netherlands, study of an
emancipation movement); Meppel/Amsterdam: Boom.
2. For the European background see: Boswell, J. (1980). *Christianity, social tolerance and homosexuality: Gay people in Western Europe from the beginning of the
Christian Era to the Fourteenth Century.* Chicago: University of Chicago Press.

3. Boon, L. (1983, June). *Those damned sodomites: Public images of sodomy in the 18th Century Netherlands.* Paper presented at the conference "Among Men, Among Women," Amsterdam.

4. See the article of Salden in this volume.

5. Salden, M. (1983, June). *Penal legislation and intimate relations among men/ among women.* Paper presented at the conference "Among Men, Among Women," Amsterdam.

6. Lijphart, A. (1968). *The politics of accommodation: Pluralism and democracy in The Netherlands.* Berkeley, CA: University of California Press.

7. See Tielman, op. cit., pp. 76-127.

8. Steakly, J. (1975). *The homosexual emancipation movement in Germany 1860-1910.* New York: Arno Press.

9. See Tielman, op. cit., pp. 110-111.

10. See Tielman, op. cit., pp. 128-138.

11. Koenders, P. (1984). *Homoseksualiteit in bezet Nederland* (Homosexuality in the occupied Netherlands). Amsterdam: SUA.

12. See Tielman, op. cit., pp. 139-172.

13. See Tielman, op. cit., pp. 173-224.

14. Straver, C. (1976). Research on homosexuality in The Netherlands. *The Netherlands Journal of Sociology, 12,* 121-137.

15. See Tielman, op. cit., pp. 225-262.

16. Waaldijk, K. (1983, June). *Freedom and equality: Alternate goals in the gay rights movement.* Paper presented at the conference "Among Men, Among Women," Amsterdam.

17. See Tielman, op. cit., p. 225.

18. See the article by Schuyf in this issue.

19. See Tielman, R. (1986). *Ethical aspects of AIDS.* Paper presented to the International AIDS Conference, Paris.

Lesbian Emancipation
in The Netherlands

Judith Schuyf
University of Utrecht

ABSTRACT. In this article the emancipation of lesbian women as a group is reviewed from a historical viewpoint. Their gradual emancipation, along with women in general, is demonstrated by the increasing alliances and support afforded to women over the years. The growth of a unified lesbian movement is evident in publications and the formation of autonomous organizations in the 20th century.

It has often been remarked that lesbian women are doubly oppressed in this world. Yet, although lesbianism is more often thought of as a source of oppression, such a lifestyle can also foster viable perspectives on liberation and emancipation.

As in other societies, lesbian women in The Netherlands are oppressed both because they are women and because they choose other women as their partners, a fact of which many lesbian women have not always been conscious. Such oppression can be both demoralizing and liberating; once insight has been gained into the mechanism of a certain situation, one can try to find a way out. This way out I call emancipation, which usually takes two directions: one seeks social equality and civil rights, the other a women's culture on its own terms—in essence, independence. The two are basically a change of structure versus a change of style. Although prerequisite for both is the development of some sort of identity, it goes beyond that: It is the idea

Judith Schuyf is the coordinator of the Interfaculty Group of Lesbian/Gay Studies at the State University of Utrecht. Correspondence may be addressed to the author, c/o the above department, Heidelberglaan 1, 3584 CS Utrecht, The Netherlands.
This article was written in 1983.

19

that one shares certain traits of this identity with other people and needs to make a political analysis of one's situation. This article deals specifically with group emancipation from a historical perspective.

The democracies in western Europe are negotiation democracies: They house many different minority interests which are bound to finding solutions by mutual arrangement. One can gain points by giving in to others. As there is no established majority, it is essential to acquire allies. Did lesbian women earlier this century indeed acquire these allies and, if so, to what end? The potential allies for lesbian women were, in fact, everyone who supported personal freedom and political emancipation politically, and in particular, the classical left: socialists and progressive liberals, whose views were opposed to those of religiously inspired political parties, and who saw the state as being primarily moralist. The most important allies were those groups with which lesbian women had something in common, women and homosexual men. Such an alliance, however, was not totally without danger. Lesbian women could enter a marriage of convenience with the gay movement or be smothered in the sisterhood of feminism.

1910 TO 1945

Homosexual contacts between adults and minors were penalized between 1911-1971 in The Netherlands (cf. Tielman, this issue). In contrast to comparable laws in other countries, Dutch law Article 248bis affected both men and women. In reality, many more men were convicted than women,[1] although the psychological effect was felt by women also; i.e., fear of blackmail and repression by police.[2] However, the most direct effect was that homosexuality was no longer an "unspeakable crime." It was brought into public discussion and was politically debated by progressives and religious groups. The debate centered on *male* homosexuality: In the discussion on 248bis nobody seemed to realize that women were also involved. Nevertheless, a number of women signed the petition Schorer organized against Article 248bis.[3] Some of them were important members of feminist organizations; however, they did not commit themselves on this matter for there was not yet any organized debate on female homosexuality.

A large number of lesbian women took part in the women's movement at the beginning of the 20th Century. We have evidence of their participation from Germany in Anna Rüling's 1904 lecture,[4] in which she noted this fact, as well as the fact that feminist women frequently disowned their lesbian sisters. "Uranian" women had done so much for the movement: "With her androgynous characteristics, she was often the one who initiated action because she felt most strongly the many, many injustices and hardships with which laws, society and archaic custom treat women." This same feeling was demonstrated by the Dutch homosexual Joannes François who remarked, in one of the first homosexual rights pamphlets of 1916, that the "striking masculinity" of the woman "who is like that" made it probable that she played an important role in the women's movement.[5]

At the same time, the article by Anna Rüling demonstrated why there was no discussion in The Netherlands between feminists and homosexuals. In Germany, lesbian women were conscious of an identity *as a lesbian,* and the form this identity took was the trademark of the German gay rights movement, Hirschfeld's Wissenschaftlich Humanitäres Kommittee (WHK), the "Third Sex." Apart from the usual two sexes, there was a third which united both homosexual men and lesbian women who shared characteristics of the opposite sex.[6] In The Netherlands, lesbian women were, primarily, *women.* Thus in the feminist magazines the discussion was about femininity. Apart from that, the feminist movement seemed inclined to follow the religious political parties in their moralist view.[7]

The Dutch Scientific Humanitarian Committee (NWHK), the

anti-Article 248bis homosexual emancipation committee, slumbered after 1911. It had always been very much a one-man show, although it formally had a board. Schorer, the committee's leader, had a very large library on homosexuality, both male and female, but apart from it the committee was of little interest to women. Even so, a number of novels with lesbian themes were published during the period 1918-1940, the so-called Interbellum. We know that Schorer stimulated women to write about lesbian themes, e.g., Anna Blaman and Marie-Louise Doudart de la Grée.[8] The most influential novel of the period was undoubtedly Radclyffe Hall's *Well of Loneliness*, a Dutch translation of which was published at the end of 1928. The popularity of this book was indicative of a paradoxical situation during this period: By this time, a large number of lesbian women seemed to recognize themselves in Stephen, the "Third Sex" heroine of the book, in contrast to the heroines of earlier Dutch books who were feminine and seemingly unaware of the existence of the third sex.

Just before the Second World War, a collection of autobiographies by homosexual men and women was published in The Netherlands in order to create some social understanding of their existence.[9] The women characters in this collection all conformed to the "third sex" model; there appeared to have been some sort of lesbian identity and a lesbian lifestyle which corresponded closely to what was known until the 1960s as the "butch-fem" lifestyle. As yet there was no lesbian subculture as such. Dutch women seemed to have met each other through mutual friends. Research into such friendship networks must yet begin, but one of the best known circles was one centered around the writers Anna Blaman, Josine Reuling and Marie-Louise Doudart de la Grée.[10]

With the introduction of universal suffrage in 1920, the élan seemed to have left the women's movement. It is remarkable that during the inter-war years there was no organized opposition to the discrepancy in the social position of men and women.

One of the most poignant examples of this discrepancy was the ban on employment of the married female civil servant, a ban which lasted until 1957. During the Interbellum, the women's movement gained both in depth and in width. It was typical of Dutch women to join organizations of their own denomination. ("Verzuiling," cf. Tielman, in this issue.) During those years there was a steady increase in the number of college students and unmarried female office employees in The Netherlands, and thus more women who were, at least potentially, economically independent. All kinds of women joined all sorts of denominational and political women's clubs. Perhaps these were not the last word in emancipation, but they all seemed to lead a certain perspective on women's independence and culture.

1945 TO THE PRESENT

During the years immediately following the end of World War II, the hope existed that a whole new Dutch society could be built, a hope soon relinquished as the traditional forces of society once again gained the upper hand and directed society's efforts toward reconstructing the country. Until the end of the 1960s, the traditional roles of men and women went unquestioned. Even now, The Netherlands has the lowest percentage of women workers of any Western society. Soon after the same war, a new homosexual rights movement was founded, the COC (cf. Tielman, this issue). The COC was, and has always been, a male-dominated and male-oriented organization, yet women were encouraged to and did join—usually up to 15% of the membership was female (and at this writing, 35%). But participation in the COC was not easy for them, for even in the early 1950s women were subordinated in society as well as in the COC. In 1953 Tine van der Velde remarked[11] that it was not very logical that women were second-rate members of a gay rights movement, as gay men were supposedly not interested enough in women to feel a need to oppress them. Thus was seen the first breach in the "third sex" theory, a breach which slowly widened until the early 1960s, when lesbian women in the COC came to see themselves primarily as *women*.[12]

Since 1961 women in the COC have regularly organized special women's days about once a year[13] and the special ping-pong night on the first Monday of each month became known among Amsterdam women as the evening for meeting other women in the COC. Despite these organized lesbian activities, lesbian women (and homosexual men) in society at large were still quite invisible. After 1964, the COC started a "dialogue" with society, prompting a few men and women to reveal their homosexuality publicly. In COC circles, however, to be acceptable to the general public meant to behave conventionally: "Homophile" men should live nicely adjusted to the male norms, lesbian women should no longer look like bull dykes but instead like normal feminine women. This was perfectly in tune with local by-laws, which forbade men and women to dress in the clothes of the opposite sex.

During the 1950s and 1960s, neither of the two movements had much to offer lesbian women. What was available to them were friendship networks and, in Amsterdam, a bar culture. In a number of bars, lesbian women were welcome together with other outsiders such as semi-criminals and coloreds, Dutch society being still predominantly white in those days. This semi-criminal *milieu* lent a very special flavor to lesbian subculture.

All this changed in the second half of the 1960s, when, together with an emerging counter-culture which claimed greater freedom for alternative lifestyles and sex, there came a "second wave" of women's liberation. Like the first emancipation wave, this second wave was at first very antagonistic toward lesbian women; partly out of ignorance, for in the beginning women's liberation was a movement of the "qualified kitchens," a very limited part of the educated and professional classes, and partly out of the time-honored fear of being labeled lesbian themselves.[14]

In contrast to the attitudes of women at the beginning of the 20th Century, the new feminists of the late 1960s openly discussed established roles of men and women and, eventually, the system of enforced heterosexuality, an issue of great interest to lesbian women and later homosexual men. For the first time, the women's and gay movements shared concern in a common issue.

Nevertheless, the 1970s saw the birth of a perfect babel of tongues. During that decade feminism grew to be a grassroots movement which promoted a "feminine way of life" opposed to male-oriented values in society, and as such it increasingly became a refuge for lesbian women, many of whom had discovered their lesbian feelings only through feminism. Many were married, middle-aged, and had children. "Lesbian" meant "feminist," "feminist" meant "lesbian" (but with the sex left out), and many older lesbians were seen as misguided, if not politically suspect. On the other hand, lesbian women resented the predominantly heterosexually oriented issues and demands in the feminist movement.

Many lesbian women used the proliferation of women's centers and women's cafés as an alternative to the COC. In the end, however, the increasing tension between heterosexual and lesbian women led to the first lesbian separatist movement, Lavender September (1971). This was the first organization in The Netherlands which did not aim for structural change, but rather for a change in style. It dissolved itself, though, once it too was labeled a structural movement. In the years that followed, all sorts of groups came into being. Among those was Group 7152, for those for whom the COC was too male-oriented, the anarchistic groups too radical, and the homosexual movement too anti-bisexual.

A counter-culture has also been available to lesbian women in the 1980s, including options such as squatting, radio-piracy and punk with either other lesbians or with heterosexual women. The counter-culture of the 1980s has also been largely a youth culture, as divisions in society developed not only between men and women, but increasingly between people above and under age 30. It has also been the culture of the second "open" lesbian generation, which has been reaping the harvest which the first generation sowed. For example, in the COC women's demands have been met within a federative structure. But the COC in the 1980s no longer is the Holy Mother Church: There are all sorts of political and professional caucuses in which lesbian women participate either with men or in some sort of federative structure. And the divisions still multiply: S/M dykes, lesbians with children, older lesbians, and so forth.

It might be that lesbian women still seek the same goal, but through various strategies. Yet one thing has become increasingly clear: Lesbian women organize themselves increasingly on their own terms. The question remains what those terms are, as demonstrated by the recent wave of publications on the "lesbian identity." Does it exist, and if so, what does it mean? What do lesbians have in common, what separates them, and why is this so? The variables in the debate are class, education, involvement in society, gender identity and role playing, and political views. It is not clear as yet what the outcome will be, but one thing is certain: Lesbian women will never return to being an invisible minority.

NOTES

1. Between 1911 and 1971, 4 women were convicted; 2 in the year 1965. Cf. Schuyf, J. (1981). Lollepotterij Geschiedenis van het "sapphisch vermaak" in Nederland tot 1940. *Homojaarboek, 1* note 4, Amsterdam; and Gezondheidsraad (1969). Advies inzake relaties met minderjarigen, in het bijzonder met betrekking tot Artikel 248bis van het Wetboek van Strafrecht. Den Haag.

2. This effect is often mentioned by women who were active in the subculture of the 1950s and 1960s. The effects on lesbians before this period are unknown.

3. NWHK: Wat iedereen behoort te weten omtrent Uranisme. Den Haag 1911. One hundred thirty persons signed the petition, of whom 19 were women.

4. Rüling, A. (1905). Welches Interesse hat die Frauenbewegung an der Lösung des homosexuellen Problems? In: Jahrbuch für sexuelle Zwischenstufen, Bd. VII, p. 131-151. Leipzig. A translation appeared in Faderman, L. & Erickson, B. (1980). Lesbian-feminism in turn-of-the-century Germany. Weatherby Lake: Naiad Press.

5. François, J.H. (1916). Open brief aan Hen, die anders zijn dan de anderen, door Eén Hunner. Den Haag.
6. See regarding the widespread influence of this notion in Germany: Kokula, I. (1981). Weibliche Homosexualität um 1900 in zeitgenossischen Dokumenten. München: Verlag Frauenoffensive.
7. Hillege, K. (1984). Mensch of voorwerp? *Homologie, 3.*
8. Tielman, R. (1981). Homoseksualiteit in Nederland. Meppel: Boom.
9. Stokvis, B. (1939). De Homoseksueelen. Lochum: De Tijdstroom. The publication of this collection was a very courageous act.
10. Kooten Niekerk, A. van & De Wit, B. (1979). Houdt de fakkel brandende. Maaike Meijer e.a.: Lesbisch Prachtboek. Amsterdam: Sara.
11. Velde, T. van der, in *Vriendschap* (COC Magazine), 1953.
12. Onstenk, A. (1983). Van brede schouders tot hoge hakken. Veranderende beeldvorming over lesbische vrouwen in de periode 1939-1965. Amsterdam: SUA.
13. Van Kooten Niekerk and De Wit, op. cit.
14. Cf. Tielman, op. cit. p. 208 for reference.

Lesbian Struggle
Against a Pillow or a Wall:
A Dutch-American Dialogue

Gail Pheterson
Leny Jansen
University of Amsterdam

ABSTRACT. A dialogue between two lesbian women is conducted in an effort to demonstrate the differences in attitude and level of tolerance towards lesbians in the United States as compared to those in The Netherlands. Their observations suggest there are positive and negative aspects to being a lesbian in both countries and they hope that the positive benefits in both countries will combine.

This shall be a dialogue between a Dutch lesbian living in Chicago and an American lesbian living in Amsterdam. When first invited to write a comparison of lesbian lives in our two countries, we felt cautious about the dangers of over-generalizing culture and lesbian life as well as of biasing our analysis with personal impressions. In order to avoid such dangers and still initiate some examination of Dutch and American lesbian contexts, we decided to abandon any attempt at scientific objectivity at this stage, and rather to speculate on cultural nuances in the interest of guiding further study. At the risk of egocentrism, we have chosen to grasp those nuances from our own cross-cultural experience.

Given the Dutch focus of this issue of the *Journal of Homo-*

Gail Pheterson is Visiting Professor of Psychology at the University of Amsterdam. Leny Jansen has a PhD in cultural history from the University of Chicago. Her dissertation entailed a cultural comparison between the Dutch and the English 17th Century social welfare systems.

29

sexuality, strongest emphasis will be put on The Netherlands with the United States as a counterpoint for cultural contrast. Both American and Dutch societies are dominated by male prerogatives and heterosexual presumptions, and in that way they are not unrepresentative of the world at large. An examination of lesbian life is therefore necessarily an examination of the specific pressures and permissions which determine the quality and quantity of struggle within each society. Such struggle is rarely unilateral, however: No one is *just* a lesbian. Every lesbian is a *woman* of a certain color, class, religion, age, language, history, culture, city or village, and so on. It is that constellation of identities within the dominant cultural setting which depicts each lesbian's experience.

The perspective of this article will reflect our personal identities and histories: Leny is 44 years old, white, middle-class, and is of a Dutch Calvinist, rural working-class background. Gail is 38 years old, white, middle-class, and is of an urban American Jewish, second-generation immigrant background.

Gail: Leny, tell something about your situation in the United States and about your experience as a lesbian.

Leny: I came to the United States to study community organizing and then history at the graduate school of the University of Chicago. My studies and a lover (I came out as a lesbian in the U.S.) were the reasons I stayed at the university and lived in the city's Hyde Park neighborhood for 10 years. One of the things that I found particularly attractive was the combination of "high power" academia and a homey neighborhood. It was an intellectually challenging environment, something I had missed in The Netherlands. Dutch society, even the university world, is far less intellectually oriented. And the racially and culturally integrated neighborhood (blacks, whites, Asians, and many foreigners) had an easy-going atmosphere in which I felt very much at home. For American standards, the neighborhood was protected and quite tolerant of differences; any behavior which could be put under the heading "eccentric" was acceptable. So, as a lesbian, I didn't have to cramp my style.

Gail: What is your impression of lesbian life beyond Hyde Park?

Leny: The minute I contemplated moving to other cities in the United States, except where there were large lesbian communities, I got scared. My impression of lesbian life beyond my neighborhood was one of strong discrimination. I couldn't be myself out there. As a lesbian I would have had to make a fist for myself in preparation either for the "barricades" or for hiding. That's the case in most American communities. The big American hero is still the tough pioneer or the rough freedom-loving cowboy who shoots everybody standing in his way, or the jock with big muscles. Those characters are the ones American men identify with and many heterosexual women cheer on. I find the images rather frightening. They set the tone of American society in general and of the relationship between men and women in particular. The struggle of lesbian women is intense and very clear. If you gain a small piece of territory in this society, it is a major achievement.

Gail: Did you have any direct experience in that realm of society or did you manage to avoid it?

Leny: I had first-hand experience. I worked for several years as a community organizer in a suburban Chicago school setting where I was definitely in the closet. Under no circumstances would I have been able to maintain my position if I had come out to my colleagues, the school board, or the community. Homophobia was rampant. And now, in my new profession in the downtown business world of Chicago, I again cannot come out without jeopardizing my job or, in any case, my opportunities for promotion.

Gail: Did you have a different experience in The Netherlands?

Leny: Yes, when I went back there for 3 years in between my studies, I was out as a lesbian at work. I never felt any threat, danger, or discomfort. I experienced tremendous toleration and openness. Not disclosing my lesbianism there would have felt like a personally neurotic choice instead of a sensible reaction to a discriminating society.

Gail: Unfortunately, discrimination in The Netherlands seems to be on the increase, if not obviously then subtly. For example, a man was rejected for a personnel position at the Dutch Royal Palace after it was discovered that he was homosexual. The stated reason for rejection was not his homosexuality but his self-concealment. Why hadn't he told that he was a homosexual? Some members of parliament claimed that such intentional concealment might indicate that the applicant was untrustworthy and posed a security risk, i.e., he would be vulnerable to blackmail. Homosexuality seems to be a threat whether revealed or concealed. Still, I'm certain that different cultures have different styles of oppression. From your exposure to both societies, Leny, how do you view the differences?

Leny: That's a broad question. I can start by telling you my view of Dutch men, which admittedly will be stereotyped and over-generalized. Rather than tough, rough, and muscled, the Dutch male hero is a mild-mannered fellow. Although the society is male and heterosexually dominated, the men are less likely than American men to come across as domineering figures. Dutch male domination is very subtle; the men are soft and pleasant. They are more family-oriented than American men, and they downplay aggressive assertion.

Gail: Are you saying that the relationship of men toward women is less offensive in The Netherlands than in the United States?

Leny: In a way, yes. There are few hard edges, but generally the exchanges seem pleasant. Nevertheless, women are dominated. Male heterosexual bias is ever-present. But it is difficult against someone who is sweet and caring; as a lesbian and feminist, you come across as a harsh bitch. When you make a fist you punch against a pillow instead of a wall. Compared to that almost unrecognizable absorbing domination, the situation in the United States is crystal clear.

Gail: In other words, lesbian oppression in The Netherlands is more subtle than in the States, but nevertheless it is present.

Leny: Yes, definitely. However, the situation is a lot more mystified. The oppression is less obvious; you can't put your finger on it. This mystification process is a quality of Dutch life in general. The Dutch tend to absorb variations from the norm instead of coughing them out. They at first accept diverse behavior instead of isolating it. Isolation encourages dissent; the Dutch apply subtle group pressure to discourage dissent and non-conformity.

Gail: If lesbians are not oppressed by being tucked in the closet, nor by losing their jobs, in what ways are they oppressed?

Leny: They are still THE LESBIANS; they are freaks. Lesbians enjoy civil rights and protections as human beings within a society which prides itself on its human decency. You are *allowed* to be a lesbian, but you have to behave like the rest of the population. If you live a life according to a lesbian-identified world view, you are a freak. *That* is unacceptable. If you give a lesbian interpretation to political events, to psychological mechanisms in human exchange, to social dynamics, you will be made to look ridiculous.

Gail: As a Dutch person, what else have you noticed about lesbian life in the United States?

Leny: As a lesbian you experience little freedom in the male heterosexual world, but you do experience great freedom of expression with other lesbians. That division may be the reason for the strong identity of lesbian women in the United States. For instance, when I go to a women-identified or lesbian cultural activity and see all those women, I rediscover my identification: "This is my world, Dyke City." The clear sense of "we women together" is extremely exhilarating. I never had such a distinct experience in The Netherlands, although I know all-women's cultural events are becoming bigger and more frequent happenings there as well. Still, my impression is that the situation there is much more diffuse. For example, my discussions with lesbian friends in The Netherlands are more about life in general than about our position as lesbians. When I meet lesbian friends in Chicago, we might talk about our personal lives, but sooner or later we will discuss the lesbian stance, lesbian experiences, lesbian horrors, and so forth. Being a lesbian is always on our minds. I am not sure whether that's the case in The Netherlands. But then perhaps I am not qualified to make that kind of observation because I lived there as a lesbian for only 3 years, and that was some time ago.

Gail: If you experience life in The Netherlands to be so much easier, why do you choose to live in the United States?

Leny: I like the clarity of the struggle, and I like identifying with an adamant, courageous lesbian stance. What about you? What has your experience been within the 2 societies?

Gail: I identify with your feelings about the clarity and intensity of the lesbian struggle in the United States. Before moving to The Netherlands, I lived openly as a lesbian for 4 years in Southern California, first as a graduate student and then as a university lecturer. My lesbian world was an activist feminist one, my work world a male-dominated heterosexual one with enclaves of academic feminists, both heterosexual and closeted lesbians. When I came out at the university by expressing indignation about the male heterosexual bias in the psychology textbooks, my department chairman warned me that I was seriously jeopardizing my professional career. At the same time, I experienced enormous pressure from my heterosexual friends and family. Associating with a lesbian was stigmatized behavior for any heterosexual, and surely for heterosexuals whose family included a lesbian. Of course, some people were more titillated than offended, but all reacted intensely. I soon realized that as an openly lesbian woman, the rest of my identity faded into the background; I had become "the lesbian," or, as you said, "the freak."

Basically, the struggle demanded a great deal of courage and was frightening for me. Yet it was also energizing and self-affirming. I wouldn't wish it on anyone, but perhaps such blatant oppression does foster the development of a strong identity. If so, that development usually occurs in isolation from the heterosexual world. When I lived in California, I considered such isolation to be a disability, and in fact, my move to The Netherlands was in part an attempt to extricate myself from that constriction.

Leny: I would like to hear more about your experience as an American lesbian in The Netherlands.

Gail: I first went to The Netherlands in 1975 to facilitate a series of feminist therapy workshops. During the introductions on the first day, I was immediately confronted with a difference between the United States and The Netherlands, or so it seemed. Of the 30 women present, the majority of whom were heterosexual feminists, many introduced themselves as married women who lived with a husband and children, but whose most intimate relationship was with a woman lover. "Wow," I thought, "it is easy to be a lesbian in The Netherlands. Lots of women, even married women, have a woman lover." I felt free and immediately concluded that The Netherlands was nearly a paradise for lesbians. I continued to glorify Dutch lesbian life there during the workshops and for about a year after I returned to live in The Netherlands. In fact, my awe of Dutch decency and naturalness grew as I learned more. I was particularly impressed with the civil liberties that lesbians and gay men had under Dutch law, and with the integration of lesbians in the women's movement, the gay movement, and heterosexual society. For example, when I first arrived in The Netherlands and needed to establish legal residency, I was amazed to learn that a stable (meaning 3-year) homosexual relationship between a foreigner and a

Dutch citizen served as a legal justification for the foreigner to remain in The Netherlands. The existence of such a legal ruling is indicative of Dutch ethics. And the Dutch do apply their ethics. For example, they went so far as to write letters, signed by members of parliament, to Florida newspapers and President Carter in the 1970s protesting the discrimination of homosexuals which was incited by Anita Bryant, and urging the government of the United States to protect human rights.

Leny: So as a lesbian you felt integrated.

Gail: Yes, more or less. And at the beginning of my residency in The Netherlands, I experienced the integration as a great relief. I suppose I was partially recovering from the painful isolation I had experienced in the United States. But after a while I began to see the dangers and freedoms of both integration and isolation.

Leny: What dangers and freedoms did you discover in the integration of Dutch lesbians?

Gail: Well, my first example is a continuation of the story of those heterosexual feminists with a husband, child(ren), and a woman lover. One certainly gets the picture of "perfect" integration, one big happy family. However, such an arrangement can be politically mystifying and personally insulting. The married woman ends up benefiting from heterosexual privilege and colluding with lesbian oppression by keeping a lesbian of her own in the closet. As a lesbian myself, I became less and less excited about the liberalism of Dutch liberty. What a mistake for me to think that if women were free to make love with other women, then they must be *free* of heterosexual bias. I had known theoretically all along, although much less so on a personal level, that sexuality is only a small part of lesbian life and of lesbian oppression. In fact, sexual license can become an excuse to discount the oppression that lesbians suffer. I would hear, "What's the big deal about being a lesbian? I sleep with women too." For a long time I questioned myself and blamed myself for making a big deal of nothing because, after all, it was easy to be a lesbian in The Netherlands. It took me years to uncover the mystification, and I still struggle with it. It doesn't feel good for the married woman either after a while because basically, in trying to get everything and fit in everywhere, she misses herself. And in any case, she gets very tired trying to keep everyone happy.

Leny: I think the situation in the United States is comparable, but one is less proud of it because the cultural pressure for harmony is less in American than in Dutch society. Granted, the pressure on women *as women* in both societies is to maintain harmony, and to feel guilty and personally responsible for all disharmony. In that way, Dutch values as a whole reinforce sexist pressures on women.

Gail: Yes, a harmony model of integration can be a mixed blessing. By the way, Dutch integration is not complete. Separatist lesbian voices do arise in The Netherlands, and they are increasing in number on a grass roots social/cultural level. But the most significant action-oriented feminism grows out of a unison of lesbians and heterosexual women. Most of those women are white, however, because Dutch society seems to claim its lesbians more than its (ex-)colonized people of color. Nonetheless, more and more lesbians of color are coming out and finding one another and they, more than their heterosexual counterparts, are active in both the white women's movement and the black women's movement(s). Heterosexual and lesbian feminists of color share the tension experienced in the United States between the struggle against racism and the struggle against sexism. So when I talk about the integration of lesbians, I am actually saying little about the integration of lesbians of *color,* or of *Jewish* lesbians, *older* lesbians, *disabled* lesbians, or so forth. I am merely referring to lesbians *as lesbians.* Many of us experience other interrelated struggles as well.

Leny: I don't know much about the activities of the Dutch political lesbians. Can you elaborate on that subject?

Gail: Just as in the United States, the political vanguard of lesbians in The Netherlands is split into the feminist movement and the homosexual movement. In the feminist one, lesbians make their primary alliance with heterosexual women; in the homosexual one, women make their primary alliance with homosexual men. In The Netherlands, the homosexual movement has a longer history than in the United States, and has a very solid integrated place in Dutch society. In fact, it has become an institutionalized organization which has a voice within the media, social services, educational institutions, and government policy. The homosexual movement in The Netherlands, therefore, is not a radical departure from mainstream Dutch society. Although the issues raised by the movement are progressive and challenging to the society, the existence of such an organization is quite Dutch. Financial support and political accountability are benefits of integration. Unfortunately, in the context of the gay movement, the word "lesbian" often disappears. We all become homosexuals, which means that women often vanish, that male homosexual assumptions are applied to women, and that, on the "positive" side, lesbian women get to slide in under the rights that gay men manage to secure for themselves. And, to note the danger as well as the freedom of integration, those *rights,* for men as well as women, are sometimes used to deny the continued presence of homophobic *attitudes.* For example, some homosexual Dutch policy-makers, satisfied with government spending on AIDS research and medical care, argue that they can best keep a low-profile on AIDS in order to avoid panic and prejudice among heterosexuals. In the United States, a shortage of funds forces homosexuals to confront prejudices in their struggle to gain financial support. I don't want to discount Dutch rights or plea for American struggle, but rather to stress that government rights do not necessarily imply public acceptance.

Leny: I agree. The integration of homosexuals in Dutch society has achieved a great deal in terms of civil liberties, but not necessarily in terms of changing values. The Dutch are proud to say that homosexuals have the same rights as heterosexuals, but that doesn't mean that the Dutch are ready to give them the same validation.

Gail: Indeed, lesbians and gay men are still an offense to the fabric of Dutch society; namely, the heterosexual nuclear family.

Leny: Exactly. The Dutch are very family-oriented. In The Netherlands, the family is not just a nurturing base, but also a primary source of male identity. Men in The Netherlands have home as well as work sources of self-expression and accomplishment, such as their gardens, their cooking, their social graces, and the like. And women are far more bound to the home than in the United States. About 50% of U.S. women work, whereas The Netherlands has one of the lowest percentages of working women in the West.

Gail: On the one hand, if men do not need to monopolize the work place because they also have another avenue of expression, the home, then lesbians—or any working women—might experience less discrimination, feel less excluded, and be less fearful of their male colleagues. On the other hand, if the taboo on working for women is greater in The Netherlands, then women might experience even more discrimination. In any case, tolerance of homosexuals does not necessarily change the basic Dutch value system, in particular around the prescribed role for women. Still, I don't want to deny the enormous importance of basic civil liberties. I'll take tolerance above abuse any day, and I am deeply impressed with Dutch society in that it has gone further than perhaps any country in the world to assure those liberties.

Leny: What have you observed about the relationship between the women's movement and the gay movement?

Gail: In The Netherlands, I can see very clearly how feminism has infiltrated and changed the gay movement, and how the Dutch gay liberation tradition has been responsible for much of the consciousness and mystification within the women's movement. Still, the gay movement is male-dominated, and the women's movement is heterosexual-dominated. In the last few years, the main cooperation I've seen between the two movements has been at demonstrations, an example being the yearly homosexual demonstration that has a strong feminist presence; and in taking common stances on certain political issues, such as an anti-discrimination law that includes women, heterosexual couples living together "out of wedlock," and homosexuals. Also, an international conference called "Among Women, Among Men: Forms of Recognition of Female and Male Relationships" was organized jointly by gay and women's studies at the university, which I considered a significant step toward augmenting lesbian visibility in both movements. The university has not been a sphere of lesbian activism, neither in gay nor women's studies. In fact, despite the growing attention at the university to homosexuality (Homostudies) and to feminism (Women's studies), the Dutch university has been only a limited source of lesbian political energy or insight. More influential have been the social services and social work educational institutions. In The Netherlands, social workers have not only been more likely than academics to be visible as lesbians, but also to champion the ideals and strategies of feminism within their work. As my cousin, Martha Becker, reminded me, social work has been strongly influenced by lesbians in the United States as well. Women such as Lillian Wald and Jane Adams were in the forefront of social work development and reform in the 19th century, and lesbians have continued to play a major role in American social work since then. But, unlike social workers in The Netherlands, those women did not fight for *lesbians*. They were leaders in their field, but closeted as lesbians. Still, the lesbian presence within social work, closeted or activist, is probably of significance.

Leny: The strength of Dutch initiative within social work, as opposed to academia, is rooted in the pragmatic tradition of the country, for in all areas there is greater concern with application than with theory. People are likely to be well-versed in ideas imported from abroad, often from the United States, but are themselves more prone to organize than to analyze. Americans certainly have a pragmatic tradition as well, but the tradition nestles alongside a fervent intellectual one.

CONCLUSION

Our observations suggest that the benefits of Dutch culture for lesbians include civil liberties, toleration, liberal social services, and integrated access to mainstream opportunities. The benefits of American culture include a context for the development of identity, an exhilarating lesbian culture, intellectual fervor, and clarity of struggle. As for the oppression, generally Dutch oppression could be characterized as mystification, and American oppression as isolation. It would be misleading, however, to posture the two societies in an even balance. It is less life-threatening to be a lesbian in The Netherlands than in the United States. At the same time, the United States seems to be a place of radical, energizing transformation. Perhaps the pressure to change basic values will come from the United States, and the pressure to protect the rights of lesbians along the way will come from The Netherlands.

Wrong Lovers
in the 19th Century Netherlands

Gert Hekma
University of Amsterdam

ABSTRACT. Various styles of "male love" occurring in the 19th century are introduced. Locations and public ordinances relating to these styles of love are discussed. The development of the homosexual role is broached along with the question of whether attitudes and laws of the 19th century were responsible in part for the development of normative expectations for homosexuality which might in turn have repressed its growth.

INTRODUCTION

At this writing I am working on a thesis on the construction of the medical concept on male homosexuality in the late 19th century Netherlands. Within the scope of this reconstruction, questions will come up as to the then occurring styles of male love. On the basis of the material I collected in the course of my research, I will broach and tentatively answer three questions. The first concerns the nature of the different styles of male love in the 19th Century. The second is about the development of the homosexual role and identity, about which research is in urgent need of additional data.[1] The third deals with the phenomenon of sexual repression: To what extent can the 19th Century be regarded as an era which set the norm for homosexuality, and in turn repressed it?[2]

Gert Hekma is a lecturer for Gay Studies in the Sociology Department of the University of Amsterdam. Correspondence may be addressed to the author, Voetboogstraat 7, 1012 XK Amsterdam, The Netherlands. The author wishes to thank Michael Dallas for his translation of the article.

This article was written in winter 1982-83.

43

The terms homosexual and homosexuality were introduced into the Dutch language through medical magazines in 1892.[3] Before other terms specified homosexual realities; some of these words were borrowed from the classical languages, while others were very Dutch: sodomite, pederast, ganymede, crimen nefandum, cynaede, bougre, friendship, flikker (fairy), schandknaap (catamite), unnatural fornication, wrong lover, and their derivations. Problems with regard to these words and their connotations will not be dealt with here.

On the basis of my material, I distinguish three lifestyles. First, the two classical western forms, pederasty and male love of comrades or, in other words the male love of boys and the male love of men, for which Gide and Whitman respectively stand as models. I will subdivide both styles into three categories. However, besides both these lifestyles, there was also a diffuse form of homosexuality: accidental, public, physical, indetermined, inclusive.

DIFFUSE HOMOSEXUALITY

This undifferentiated form of homosexuality occurred in the street, in parks, on ramparts, in exclusively male societies such as prisons, monasteries, and armies, on ships, at boarding schools, and it was often a pursuit at any type of men's gathering. The relations concerned were characterized by a strong emphasis on physical contacts, and were of accidental nature, not lasting and not determined by particular sexual fantasies or by sexual identifications. Maybe there was a youth cult, but the dominating position of younger men in this form of homosexuality was probably the result of their lack of sexual discipline and the absence of women in their lives. Men married late and, besides, marriage was not the general rule in The Netherlands of the 19th Century.[4] It is this form of homosexuality to which the legal archives rather abundantly bear testimony, and against which the responsible authorities proceeded with increasing strictness.[5] The transition from collective detention to solitary confinement during this period was probably prompted by the "profligacy" of the prisoners, and resulted in various measures being taken in the prison dormitories, such as installation of more lighting, a different formation for sleeping mats, and more warders. Yet these scarcely had any effect.[6] There is little information available about sexual conduct on Dutch ships. However, they did play an important role in the great debate about medical regulations regarding prostitution. Those who fought prostitution asserted that the Dutch sailors were paragons of chastity,[7] whereas their opponents claimed the very opposite, labeling the sailors as "thousands, who either privately, or secretly with someone of the same sex, satisfy their lusts."[8] The first homosexual case concerned a naval officer who, after his dismissal from the navy, sent his "autobiography" to C. Winkler, professor of psychiatry, which P. F. Spaink published in 1893 in the *Psychiatrische Bladen* (Psychiatric Papers).[3] On every voyage this officer had had sexual adventures with many (once as many as 30) members of the crew, some of whom were regular partners. The officer labeled only a minority of his partners "uranians."[9]

In the streets of the late 19th century Netherlands men had sexual contacts which often were of an accidental and transitory nature. From the legal archives, it appears that now and again there were regular relationships and regular "cottagers," people who frequented cottages, i.e., public conveniences. Furthermore, there were boys and men who, without much ado, satisfied their sexual lusts with men they met in the street or in public conveniences. Toward the end of the century these diffuse, informal forms of homosexuality were increasingly dealt with by the police.[10] For legal authority to discourage such behavior, labeled as outrage to the public decency, the police appealed to paragraph 330 of the French Penal Code, operative in The Netherlands from 1811 to 1886, and Article 239 of the Dutch Criminal code, in effect since 1886.

The modernization of the public conveniences halfway into the 19th century was an additional obstacle to sexual contacts. Before the modernization took place, public conveniences were found under bridges, in the dark, and were only accessible via a flight of stone stairs. Some juridical reports of the period talk of night watchmen who claimed they first took off their (wooden) shoes before descending to the convenience under the bridge, so that they could catch wrong lovers in the act. At the end of the 19th Century, lights were placed over the urinals and sidewalls were constructed in a way that made it easy to assess from the outside what the urinal was actually being used for.[11]

The homosexual needs of a great many men appear to have been satisfied irregularly; they were direct, physical, accidental, not exclusive, and were often fulfilled in a more or less public place. Because the sexual desires of other men were more differentiated, they required a higher degree of homosexual organization.

MALE LOVE OF COMRADES

The three principal forms of the male love of comrades were the following:

1. At the end of the 19th century there was a number of meeting places for sodomites in beer and coffeehouses in Amsterdam.[12] From closer inquiry it appears that similar meeting places existed at the beginning of the 18th century.[13] Data about the intervening period are as yet not available. The police raids on these public houses were, as far as I know, without juridical consequence.[14] According to the Dutch criminal law these places were legitimate. Police actions were justified only on the ground of by-laws or in the event of incitement of fornication with

minors. It does not appear unlikely to me, if the police raids were mainly meant to hinder the functioning of such meeting places.

The most comprehensive information about such a beerhouse we owe to a gutter-press journalist called Abraham Cornelisse. In 1897 he launched a campaign against George Hermans' beer house on Smaksteeg, which, for clarity's sake, he called "Sodom-Societeit." He did not stop at words only, but even threw in the windows of the cafe. This "sodomite" was not only the proprietor of a pub, but also a doctor of secret or venereal diseases, so a quack and a labor-broker into the bargain. This way he had various possibilities "to give rein to his debauched lusts." In his newspaper Cornelisse described the interior of the place: many flowers and portraits of the members of the royal family.[15]

2. These beerhouses were without doubt also places where male prostitutes could be bought and there must have been a close link with brothels, which will be discussed later. But they certainly served as places where "wrong lovers" could meet one another. Beside this possibility, the circle of sodomites was an important 19th century way of organizing homosexuals. In a discussion by the "Nederlandsche Vereeniging voor Psychiatrie" (The Dutch Association for Psychiatry) about uranism Professor C. Winkler made mention of unions in the larger Dutch cities that in some cases counted up to eighty uranians.[16] In 1881 the Amsterdam police caught a group of nineteen committers of "unnatural fornication" at a blow, who were nevertheless not summoned. They were all working-class men who varied in age from 18 to 67.[17]

Neither could I find much information about male couples, probably for the same reason: There was no provision against them. Or else, these sodomites thoroughly covered up their sexual lusts. Yet, as indicated by archives which chronicled prosecutions on the grounds of outrage to public decency, some men concerned appeared to meet each other regularly at the same spot. In 1833 nightwatches arrested a chemist's assistant and a stage walk-on who had been kissing and caressing one another between 12 and 1 a.m. at the same streetcorner for a fortnight. The nightwatches had been chasing them for two weeks before finally succeeding to arrest them.[18] In 1864 alarmed citizens caught two sodomites who for nights on end had been spending one or two hours in a public convenience and had left it before the arrival of the nightwatches patrolling the bridge. A woman who dealt in pickles and eggs near the public convenience was the first to report their activities, for the sodomites had bought food from her before their cozy gathering.[19]

Only one case of friends living together has come to my attention. A witness testified before the Committee of Prostitution of Amsterdam City council "that on the third floor of a brothel, at night and right in front of the window, two men are powdering and caressing each other. The vice these men commit . . . (is) too obvious. . . ."[20] These homosexual affairs lasted longer, were more regular, more exclusive, often less public, and probably more determined by sexual preference and identities than the contacts made in the street.

3. A last variation was the romantic friendships that developed between students and other men, especially during the Romantic Period. In the 19th century Netherlands, passionate but chaste relationships must have occurred frequently, for in the corporate life of students they were generally a socially appreciated phenomenon. Well-known examples of these chaste relationships are evident in the group known as the "reverend poets" (they were protestant priests) who studied in Leiden in the 1830s[21] and within the literary movement of the 1880s in Amsterdam.[22] These relationships sometimes were of an extremely homo-erotic nature. In Leiden one of the friends was called "Jonathan," and the poetic caprices of W. Kloos, a representative of the movement of the 1880s, were overtly homosexual, whereas later on this poet quenched his desires with alcohol and marriage. Among the various lifestyles, all sorts of transitions were possible. A man could praise romantic

friendships to the sky and at the same time be an active "cottager." These transitions also took place between the love comrades had for one another, as well as between the love some men had for boys.

FROM PEDERASTY TO PEDAGOGIC EROS

Lads and boys have not always been the submissive objects of male adults' lust. From the persecution records of the police, it is evident that boys from the age of 9 seduced other boys their own age and were held at least partly responsible by the justice for their deeds. Usually, however, the public prosecutor did not prosecute cases of homosexual fornication between boys under the age of 16 nor prosecute boys who were involved in pederastic relations. Yet the policies of justice and public prosecution seem to have been rather arbitrary, for lawyers were entangled in the ideology of the innocent child and the responsible adult. As a result, children potentially could become legally responsible adults somewhere between the ages of 9 and 23.[23]

Some pederastic affairs included a financial transaction. Sometimes the boys offered themselves for free, while other times they charged a few cents up to a maximum of a "rijksdaalder" (half a week's pay for an errand boy). In the 19th Century sexuality was closely linked with money. Prostitution had assumed large proportions and so had pederasty.

1. Just as there were different types of male love between comrades, so were there different types of pederasty. First, there was male prostitution in the streets, sometimes spread all over the town, sometimes at one spot. Around 1900 Kalverstraat, an Amsterdam street which borders on Munt, was where hustlers sold their love.[24] On the same street the "Tijdingzaal," hall where the latest newspapers could be read, was probably a place where boys traded their beauty for money. By the end of the 19th Century, there were, besides male streetwalkers, boys

who worked in the brothels of Amsterdam, Arnhem, and The Hague. The word brothel is perhaps an exaggeration, though, considering the simple facilities the houses offered their customers. Such a brothel in The Hague is the only place about which we have clear information. It was a back room in a tobacco shop in which men mutually masturbated with boys whom they paid.[25] "De Middernachtzending" (the Midnight Mission), a society that fought prostitution, drew up a list of brothels in Amsterdam, including 5 places most of which seem to have been normal houses. One of the brothel keepers was later sentenced on the charge of inciting fornication with minors, nota bene, committed out of the house. To seduce boys he used pornography, and he confessed to having joined in public feasts dressed up like a woman.[26] In another instance, police raided a brothel in Arnhem and found 40 customers there, all of whom were later released.[27]

The brothels served yet other important functions for the subculture of wrong lovers as well. In a number of cases, the brothel keepers worked as agents in foreign real estate, which enabled them to house rich customers abroad in the event of a scandal or a criminal case, and as pimps, labor-broker, which enabled them to recruit new boys and get rid of boys who had served their time. For the pederastically inclined, these brothels no doubt formed the nerve center of the subculture by virtue of their various functions.

2. The fact that brothel keepers also lent boys out on contract served yet another purpose. Well-to-do sodomites could employ their lovers as coachmen, valets, or secretaries. It is possible that they selected their staff through these brothel keepers. But there were also different relationships that were based on dependence. In a 1904 novel, a teacher is described who carried off a carpenter's apprentice and paid him a full-time salary in order to satisfy his lusts.[29] Labor was cheap, which meant that the richer pederasts need not go to much trouble to fulfill their needs. The legal archives bear out the fact that there were men who sent for boys at set times. These relationships were punishable under the

article of the penal code concerning the promotion of fornication by minors, but were difficult to prosecute due to lack of proof of such sexual acts and their frequency, proof which required the testimonies of more than one boy, or else the defendant's confession. Laws passed in 1911 helped to facilitate prosecution of such acts, when every single act of fornication with a minor became punishable.

3. Purely romantic and aesthetic relationships not only existed between adult men, as we saw earlier, but also between an adult and a boy. In the well-established tradition of platonic pedagogy F. Hemsterhuis, P. de Raadt, P. van Heusde, and J. Kneppelhout based their philosophical systems on warm friendships. While Hemsterhuis, an influential philosopher of Romanticism, protested strongly against pederasty in his "Lettre sur les desirs" (1770) (Letter on the Desires), as far as I know the other authors left it undiscussed. Kneppelhout was without doubt an important representative of platonic pedagogy, maybe not so much for his publication of "L'education par l'amitie" (1835) as for pedagogic projects: He backed young budding artists, and contributed to the development of gymnastics in The Netherlands. Unfortunately, his most important protégés died young.[31] At least once, rumor went, Kneppelhout got so carried away by the weal and woe of his prodigies that he committed unnatural fornication with one of them.[32] De Raadt's school closed down prematurely, be it after his death, owing to an "unspeakable evil, which is so easily actuated by boarding-school."[33]

A HOMOSEXUAL ROLE AND IDENTITY?

In the 19th Century Netherlands various homoerotic lifestyles were possible. At the end of the 19th Century, medical doctors began to regard the diffuse forms of homosexuality as pseudo-homosexuality, since in their eyes it arose from necessity. It is my assumption that although the homosexual role, including the rituals of transvestism and a special jargon, was developed around brothels and beer and coffee houses, it also dated back further, certainly to the beginning of the 18th Century. When toward the end of the 19th Century medical doctors formulated the "homosexual identity," they intended it to be the identity of someone who did not need to behave himself sexually. Thus, the sodomite was characterized by his sexual conduct, the "homosexual" by his sexual continence. Torn between the temptation of the cafes and the respectability of romantic asceticism, male couples and male friends were probably those who identified with this form of homosexuality. On the one hand, men who frequented beer and coffee houses were too carnal for the chaste homosexuals, while on the other hand, romantic friends did not want to tarnish their friendship with the sexual element of homosexuality. The first Dutch works on homosexual emancipation from the beginning of this century clearly were written by middle-class citizens who called themselves homosexuals, yearned for a steady friendship, and resisted the lascivious life of "cottagers" and cafe patrons.[34] The homosexual identity was a Pyrrhus victory for middle-class homosexuals who were in agreement with the medical doctors and held very ambivalent views as to the sexual element of homosexuality. Due to their name "homosexual," not uranian or invert, these men were prisoners of an ambiguity; the wish to remain chaste and the enticement of eroticism. These men, who at least in The Netherlands formerly utilized the terminology that belonged to the realm of uranism and was derived from the classics, had been brought under the yoke of the quasi-scientific jargon of homosexuality.[35] Moreover, the active persecution of the diffuse and public forms of homosexuality stimulated the development of a hidden subculture of exclusive homosexuality.

The sodomites and pederasts who were a part of the homosexual subculture which was developing through brothels and cafés despised those grouped under the homosexual identity. Those involved in romantic and pedagogic friendships, in turn, loathed any homosexual term. But at the end of the 19th Century something else happened. In their definitions of homosexual love, doctors and homosexuals tried to avoid any association with pederasty, both in the sense of anal contacts and love for boys. Around 1900, a gap grew between male love of comrades and pederastic love. In The Netherlands, the distinction was politically and criminally sanctioned by the introduction of Article 248bis, which penalized adults who fornicated with minors of the same sex. Even a progressive instruction book on sexuality gratuitously adopted this morally colored distinction. The section on homosexuality offered no information, but foremost a warning against the dirty pederastic seducer.[36] Homosexual emancipation may have been so successful in The Netherlands because at an early stage it already was looked upon as something quite different from pederasty and anal contacts.[37]

VICTORIAN TIMES?

The notion that the 19th Century was an era of sexual repression cannot be applied to the histories of England, France, or The Netherlands. However, toward the end of the century a "purity crusade" was launched.[38] Called a sexual revolution by many,[39] this crusade primarily fought prostitution, although homosexuality also became one of its targets. These forms of sexuality, which were unspeakable before in 1880, could be talked about after that time; however, such increased openness inhibited their practice. The very fact that "unnatural fornication" was unspeakable seems to have afforded room for homosexual practices. The design of the public conveniences, the architecture of prisons, a particular fashion, flap-trousers, and the existence of all-male communities were all factors which stimulated homosexual conduct. In the second half of the 19th Century a modern, sometimes scientific, rationality repudiated these diffuse forms of homosexuality. The Sadean appeal to approach the sexual question with reason failed.[40] Rousseau's philosophy, which was based on nature and procreation, was triumphant, and reason made extra-marital sexuality its enemy. By the end of the 19th Century, all non-marital forms of sexuality could be discussed: cohabitation, prostitution, pornography, homosexuality. At the same time, sexuality was regarded as something depraved by all the movements which grew up after and thanks to liberalism, i.e., orthodox christians, socialists, and feminists. Why talking about sexuality continued to be a taboo in the new realm of human reason, and why it remained a reprobate subject for a new middle-class, and for socialists and feminists in particular, is a valuable question to explore in light of the influence it has had on the development of present-day thinking regarding sexuality.

NOTES

1. McIntosh, M. (1981). "The homosexual role." In Plummer, K. (Ed.), *The making of the modern homosexual.* London: Hutchinson; Foucault, M. (1976). *Histoire de la sexualite: La volonté de savoir.* Paris; Gallimard.

2. Cf Foucault, M., Ibid., Chapter II; van Ussel, J. M. W.: *Geschiendenis van sexuele probleem,* (Meppel 1968), Chapter XI.

3. *Geneeskundige Courant,* July 8, 1892, and *Nederlands Tijdschrift Voor Geneeskunde* 1892: II, pp. 585-588.

4. Hofstee, E. W. (1978). *De demografische ontiwikkeling van Nederland in de eerste halft van de negentiende eeuw.* NIDI, 2, p. 202.

5. Inquiry into the archives of the district courts of Amsterdam 1830-1909 and The Hague 1870-1909. I will always refer to the general prosecutor's register.

6. See Peterson, M. A. (1978). *Gedetineerden onder dak.* Leiden, n.p.

7. See e.g., H. K. (1883, March). "Is ontucht noodzakelijk?" *Getuigen en Redden, 5,* 44-45.

8. Overbeek de Meijer, G. van (1892). "Boekaankondiging." *Nederlands Tijdschrift voor Geneeskunde, 2,* 422.

9. Spaink, P. F. (1893). "Bijdrage tot de casuistiek der urningen. *Psychiatrische Bladen, XI.* "Uranians," derived from Venus Uranios, the tutelary goddess of homosexual love in Greek mythology.

10. Number of convictions in Amsterdam, 1830-1839: 10; 1840-1849: 7; 1850-1859: 7; 1860-1869: 12; 1870-1879: 27; 1880-1889: 23; 1890-1899: 48; and 1900-1909: 89.

11. See Hekma, G. (1982). Profeten op papier, pioniers op pad. *Spiegel Historiael, 17*(11), 567.

12. Ibid., p. 570.

13. Boon, L. J. (1982). "Utrechtenaren": De sodomietenprocessen in Utrecht, 1730-1732. *Spiegel Historiael*, *17*(11), 553.

14. Cf. list of brothels under the heading "sodomie" of the Prostitie-Commissie den November 6, 1895. Municipal Archives of Amsterdam, 5136.

15. *De Amsterdamse Lantaarn, weekblad voor het volk, (1897)*. *1*(1). See also "onthullingen uit de Sodom-Societeit," a pamphlet, Amsterdam 1897, Municipal Archives of Amsterdam, B (1897) 1.

16. *Psychiatrische bladen*. (1893). *XI*, 140.

17. District court of Amsterdam, 1881: Nr. 2737.

18. Ibid., 1833: Nr. 64

19. Ibid., 1864: Nr. 1116.

20. See note 14.

21. Kneppelhout, J. (1835). L'education par l'amite: *Opvoeding door vriendschap, toegelicht door Marita Mathijsen en Frank Ligtvoet*. The Hague: van Stockum.

22. About Kloos and his friends, van Eeten, P. (1963). *Dichterlijk Labyrint*, Amsterdam: Polak en Van Gennep.

23. Smidt, H. J. (1881). "23 jaar vgl. debatten over koppelarij-artikel Wetboek Van Strafrecht." *Geschiedenis van het Wetboek van Strafrecht*, 2, Haarlem.

24. Hirschfeld, M. (1914). *Die homosexualitat des mannes und des weibes*. Berlin: Marcus.

25. District court of the Hague, 1900: 847.

26. District court of Amsterdam, 1904: 3166.

27. The monthly *Getuigen en Redden*, March 1897, p. 23.

28. From comparison with the *Amsterdamsch Andresboek* concerning this period of time.

29. De Haan, J. I. (1904). *Pijpelijntjes*. Amsterdam: *Van Cleef*.

30. See Salden, M. (1980). "Artikel 248bis Wetboek van Strafrecht." *Groniek*, 66.

31. Kneppelhout, J. (1980). *Opvoeding door vriendschap* (see note 21), pp. 43-48.

32. Kneppelhout, J. (1875). *Een beroemde knaap*. The Hague: Nijhoff.

33. *Gedenkboek Noorthey*, (1920), Haarlem (without pagination).

34. E. g., Exler, M. J. J. (1911). *Levensleed*, The Hague, Heezen, C. van (1918). *Anders*, The Hague, and Luctor et Emergo (1922). *Het Masker*, The Hague; Brondgeest, B. (1921). *Doolhof*, Amsterdam: Querido.

35. Aletrino, A. (1908). *Hermaphrodisie en Uranisme*, Amsterdam: Van Rossen; and under the pen-name Ihlfeld, K. (1905). *Over Uranisme*, Amsterdam: Tierie; von Roemer, L. S. A. M. (1905). *Het Uranisch Gezin* Amsterdam: Tierie; NWHK (1912). *Wat iedereen behoort te weten omtrent uranisme*, The Hague: n.p.

36. Premsela, B. (1934). *Geslachtelijke voorlichting voor de rijpere jeugd*. Amsterdam: Mulder & Co.

37. Article 248bis repudiated pederasty, c.f., also previous note. About anal sex, c.f., Aletrino, A. (1987). Over uranisme en het laatste werk van Raffalovich, *Psychiatrische en Neurologische Bladen, I*, 453.

38. C.f., Pivar, D. J. (1973). *Purity crusade, sexual morality and control, 1868-1900*, London: Westport.

39. C.f., van Ussel, J. M. W. (1968). *Geschiedenis van get sexuale probleem*. Meppel: Boom.

40. Particularly De Sade, D. A. F. (1795). *La philosophie dans le boudoir*. London: n.p.

Constitutional Protection Against Discrimination of Homosexuals

Kees Waaldijk
University of Limburg

ABSTRACT. A brief review of equality for homosexuals prior to 1983 is presented followed by the introduction and explanation of the relevant section of the revised edition of the Dutch Constitution (enacted in 1983). The possible impact of this section on the abolishment of discrimination based on sex and sexual orientation is discussed.

EQUALITY BEFORE 1983

"All people who are on the territory of the State, have an equal claim to protection of person and goods." These words could be read in the Dutch constitution from 1815 till 1983.[1] The Dutch Supreme Court[2] however, hardly ever invoked them. This does not mean that the notion of equal protection has been legally unimportant in The Netherlands, for, in fact, the principles of equal protection of the various religions can be seen as one of the roots of this state. But equal protection has never been as major a legal topic in The Netherlands as we are told it its in the United States. This can in part be explained by the fact that the judiciary in The Netherlands does not check the constitutionality of parliamentary legislation; this is left to parliament itself. Unconstitutional statutes are valid and binding. Therefore, not only is the equal protection clause not a major theme in Dutch law, but the

---

Kees Waaldijk is a lecturer in the Department of Public Law at the University of Limburg, and was coordinator of the National Working Group on Legislation of the COC. Correspondence may be addressed to the author, Faculty of Law, Rijksuniversiteit Limburg, Postbus 616, 6200 MD Maastricht, The Netherlands.

whole constitution as a legal instrument is not as important as it is in the United States, where judges do review the constitutionality of statutes. Even where judicial control or constitutionality is possible, i.e., where laws made by bodies other than parliament are concerned, equal protection has not been a frequently discussed topic. The recently increasing attention paid in The Netherlands to the notions of equality and non-discrimination could be partly explained by the political emergence of new groups of the population: colored people from former colonies, migrant workers, feminists, and gay people.

EQUALITY SINCE 1983

All persons in the Netherlands shall be treated equally in equal circumstances. Discrimination on the grounds of religion, belief, political opinion, race or sex or on any grounds whatsoever shall not be permitted.

Since 1983 these have been the opening words of the completely revised Dutch constitution.[3]

This change in the constitutional wording of the principle of equality can be seen as a result of the increasing concern for non-discrimination, referred to in the first paragraph. It is as yet uncertain whether this new phrasing will have much impact on legal discussions, in court or elsewhere.

It should be noted that the Dutch Constitution after the 1983 revision still forbids judicial review of acts of Parliament. In this direction the importance of the Constitution will not increase. Nevertheless, there are two features of the revised Constitution which allow for some speculation about the growing constitutionalization of human rights in The Netherlands. First, the revised Constitution opens with a systematic catalogue of no less then 23 human rights, which is more than the rights which were scattered in various paragraphs of the Constitution in its pre-1983 text. This increased constitutional attention for human rights has been accompanied by an increase in the quantity of legal writing on the subject. One would expect this would lead those in government and those controlling or criticizing the government to take constitutionally protected human rights more often into account. Several examples of such increasing constitutionalism may already be noticed, one being that in discussions between government authorities and the gay movement both parties now frequently refer to the new non-discrimination clause.

Second, during the parliamentary debates leading to the recent revisions of the Constitution, the legislature (i.e., both Government and Parliament) made it clear that the scope of human rights must not be confined only to so called vertical relations between citizens and government authorities. Therefore, it is possible and likely that both the courts and the legislature will apply constitutionally protected human rights to so-called horizontal relations between citizens. A controversial example of this can be found in a proposal by the government to forbid citizens and private institutions from discriminating between men and women, heterosexuals and homosexuals, married and unmarried people. (This proposal will be discussed later in this article.)

"OR ANY OTHER GROUNDS WHATSOEVER"

"All persons in the Netherlands shall be treated equally in equal circumstances. Discrimination on the grounds of religion, belief, political opinion, race or sex shall not be permitted."

This was the text of the original government proposal for a constitutional phrasing of the principle of equality,[4] a proposal which caused critical comments both in the Council of State[5] and in the Parliament. The text was said to suggest that discrimination on grounds other than those named was still permitted. It was especially regretted that discrimination on account of homosexuality was not covered in the proposal. The possibility of adding "sexual orientation" as a sixth ground was rejected because that would leave other forms of discrimination uncovered and therefore permitted. Eventually, Government and Parliament agreed on adding the words "or any other grounds whatsoever."

This amendment to the original proposal brought the Dutch Constitution into line with several international treaties to which The Netherlands is a party. The International Covenant on Civil Political Rights, for example, provides that "the law shall prohibit any discrimination and guarentee to all persons equal and effective protection against discrimination on any ground such as. . .or other status."[6] Unlike the history of the International Covenant, the legislative history of the amendment to the original proposal for the revised Dutch Constitution leaves it beyond doubt that the Constitution regards sexual orientation as an "other ground" referred to in the non-discrimination clause.

A SPECIES OF SEX DISCRIMINATION

"By *discrimination on account of sex* is also understood discriminating on account of behavior or expressions contrary to qualities or characteristics ascribed to the sex of the person(s) involved."[7]

In 1977 the Government Advisory Committee on the Emancipation of Women proposed making a law against all forms of discrimination on account of sex, i.e., being male or female, including those referred to in this complex formula. If one considers the tendency to fall in love with men as a "characteristic" traditionally ascribed to women, and the tendency to fall in love with women as a "characteristic" traditionally ascribed to men, then discrimination on account of homosexuality can be viewed as a form of discrimination on account of sex. A similar line of thought has been tried in the Congress of the United States during the debates concerning the Equal Rights Amendment, and in the United Kingdom in several court cases under the Sex Discrimination Act. This line of thought, however, was adopted by neither the U.S. Legislature nor the U.K. Judiciary.[8] Although this approach was not generally adopted in The Netherlands, it nevertheless has had some impact: discrimination because of sex and discrimination because of sexual orientation are now widely seen as related forms of discrimination. Plans are being developed for a statute prohibiting both sex discrimination and sexual orientation discrimination. The Dutch gay movement stresses this link because of the common roots of the oppression of women and homosexuals.

THE COURTS

"Plaintiff has not been dismissed because of a characteristic she was afflicted with, but she was dismissed because of acts and behavior on her part."[9] For this reason a lower judge accepted the contested dismissal of a woman employee who had openly begun a love affair with one of her female colleagues. At this writing this is the most recent (1972) known case in which a Dutch judge allowed discrimination on account of homosexuality. He clearly made a distinction between a homosexual disposition and homosexual behavior, only the latter justifying dismissal.

Cases involving discrimination against homosexuals are very rare in Dutch law.[10] Therefore, it is not predictable what judges will say when they hear such a case. In 1982 an appeal court decided that a homosexual disposition as such could not be regarded as a disease or defect justifying dismissal.[11] Whether dismissal because of homosexual behavior or relations will still be accepted by courts is unknown. This underlines the importance of an Equal Treatment Act forbidding not only discrimination on account of homosexual disposition, but also discrimination on account of homosexual behavior. The number of people discriminated against on these grounds by far exceeds the number of

court cases involving discrimination against gays, a phenomenon explained perhaps by the negative decisions courts have
handed down in earlier decades. Homosexuals who are discriminated against seem to have more faith in political activity or use
of publicity as means of seeking redress; that is; if they are
already emancipated enough to seek redress in the first place.

A PARLIAMENTARY DESIRE

"To introduce a bill aimed against all types of discrimination
on account of sex (including discrimination on account of homosexuality) and of discrimination on account of marital status."[12]
This is what more than 90% of the members of the Dutch
Chamber of Representatives asked the government to do in
1978. The government responded by establishing two commit-
tees of civil servants. The first was to prepare a bill against sex
discrimination, the second to examine the consequences of and
the possibilities for a prohibition of discrimination on account of
homosexuality.

A PINK GOVERNMENT REPORT

"The fundamental conclusion is, on the one hand, that the
social opposition against homosexuality has considerably diminished, on the other hand, that actual discrimination on account of
homosexuality still occurs on a large scale."[13] So concluded the
second government committee mentioned above. Thus, the committee resolved that a legal prohibition of discrimination on account of homosexuality was both socially acceptable and socially
necessary. The government used the report of the committee
during the preparation of the draft of the Equal Treatment Act to
be discussed in the next paragraph. The report was published by
the government in a pink cover.

A DRAFT TREATMENT ACT

"Considering that the attainment of a general recognition of the equivalence of people in society will be highly served if unjustified discrimination between persons on account of sex, homosexuality or marital status is counteracted in social life and public administration,"[14] the Dutch government published in 1981 a preliminary draft of an Equal Treatment Act.

Not yet a bill introduced in Parliament, but an idea put forward by the government so that all members of society could express their thoughts about it, the draft indeed created a lot of reactions. The proposal consisted of a new statute prohibiting, in general, *unreasonable* differential treatment on account of sex, homosexuality (including behavior), marital status, or family responsibility, and prohibiting, in particular, all differential treatment on these grounds in certain well-defined areas. Those areas included labor, education, trade, and public administration. Certain fields were excluded from the general or the specific prohibitions of discrimination, including religion, emanicpation movements of women or homosexuals, private life, and scientific research. The act would be concerned only with discriminatory treatment, whereas discriminatory expressions would be covered by a proposed criminal law prohibiting incitement of sexual violence, hatred, or discrimination. People who commit any kind of discrimination prohibited by the Equal Treatment Act would be liable to the general sanctions of civil or administrative law, or both, applicable to the field in which the discrimination occurred. The draft did not provide specific new sanctions, criminal or otherwise. The proposed act, however, was to establish a Commission for Equal Treatment, whose task would be to look into cases of forbidden discrimination and give its opinion about them, as well as to mediate between the discriminators and those discriminated against. The published and unpublished opinions of the commission, however, would not be binding.

This whole preliminary draft was an elaboration of some of the existing laws relating to equal treatment of men and women in the field of labor. The European Economic Community obliged the Dutch legislature to make those laws during the 1970s. The new act, if enacted, would have a wider scope, covering more grounds (including homosexuality) and more fields of social life. At this writing Norway is the only European country with specific legislation against discrimination of homosexuals.[15] (France enacted a similar law in 1985.)

COLLIDING CONSTITUTIONAL RIGHTS

Critical reactions to the preliminary draft of an Equal Treatment Act came from very different directions. Several emancipation groups criticized the fact that discrimination against paedophilia, transvestism, and so forth was not included in the draft. Some religious groups, on the other hand, strongly objected to the narrow exception for religious activities, holding the view that all religiously inspired activities should be exempted from a legal prohibition of discrimination on account of homosexuality. The draft only provided an exemption for activities directly related to religious worship. This criticism developed into a hot political issue focusing on the "right" of christian schools to refuse to employ homosexual teachers, the main problem the government has to solve before it can introduce a final Equal Treatment Bill in Parliament. The state-funded private religious educational system is one of the traditional political strongholds in Dutch society. In addition, the freedom of parents to organize their own schools for their children is constitutionally protected.[16]

Here again emerges the importance of the new first article to the Dutch Constitution. When two rights collide, e.g., the right not to be discriminated against and the right to be master of one's own school, it is of at least symbolic importance that not only one but both of the rights are constitutional rights. In the Dutch legal system, this balancing of constitutional rights is mainly a task for the political bodies, the Government and Parliament. The text of the Constitution before 1983 did not clearly forbid discrimination against homosexuals; since 1983 it does. A balance is thereby restored between groups which won constitutional protection at the end of the last century, i.e., christian parents of school-age children, and groups which won constitutional protection during the 1970s and 1980s, i.e., gays, women, and so forth. The Dutch constitution does not solve this conflict of interests, but it does give equal support to different groups. Whether denominational schools will, in the end, be forbidden to refuse to employ homosexual teachers on the basis of their sexual preference depends on the outcome of political discussions, not on mere interpretation of the Constitution.[17]

DISCRIMINATING STATUTES

"What is laid down in this act is not applicable to discrimination contained in any other act."[18] This provision is contained in the preliminary draft of the Equal Treatment Act. It was much criticized, but probably will also be included in a final Equal Treatment Act. It implies that all discrimination based on acts of Parliament will still be legal after the Equal Treatment Act comes into force. As mentioned earlier, statutes containing unconstitutional discrimination cannot be declared void by Dutch courts.[19] For that reason, neither the new non-discrimination clause in the constitution, nor a prospective Equal Treatment Act including a prohibition of discrimination against homosexuals will guarantee that all existing statutes which discriminate against homosexuals will be changed. All hopes in that regard have to be placed on political forces in the legislative process.[20] The statute which most explicitly discriminated against homosexuals was abolished in 1971. Until then that statute had made it a criminal offense for adults to engage in homosexual acts with people between 16 and 21 years of age.[21]

A HOMOSEXUAL MARRIAGE?

"The man can at the same time only with one woman, and the woman only with one man be united in marriage."[22] This section of the Dutch Civil Code is supposed to exclude homosexual marriage. Whether or not one sees marriage as a valuable institution, it seems obvious that the legal impossibility of a homosexual marriage clearly contradicts the revised Dutch constitution. Since the courts can do nothing about this type of unconstitutional discrimination, the only way of abolishing it is by legislation. Yet it is unlikely a law will be passed on this point. First, it is not a topic at all in Dutch politics. Second, there are strong potential opponents against the idea of a homosexual marriage, especially in orthodox religious circles. And third, the national committee of the main Dutch gay organizations, the COC, has declared the possibility of marriage for homosexuals just as undesirable as the whole institution of marriage. The gay movement does play a role in the movement for equal rights for non-marital and marital relations, and a more active role in the movement for equal rights for people with and without permanent domestic relations. This is considered more important than a lobby for homosexual marriage. In these political campaigns the constitutional non-discrimination clause can be invoked. Yet it seldom is.

CONCLUSION

The Dutch Constitution, by prohibiting all discrimination on any ground whatsoever, forbids discrimination because of homosexuality. This constitutional provison has not had many direct legal consequences. The effects of the constitutional prohibition of discrimination largely depend on political forces. The new first article of the Constitution can both inspire and legitimate those political forces aiming at an Equal Treatment Act prohibiting in some detail discrimination against homosexuals in various fields of social life, and those forces aiming at an abolition of all statutory discrimination against homosexuals and unmarried people.

NOTES

1. "Allen die zich op het grondgebied van het Rijk bevinden, hebben gelÿke aanspraak op bescherming van persoon en goed." Section 4 of the Dutch Constitution before 1983.
2. Hoge Raad.
3. "Allen die zich in Nederland bevinden, worden in gelÿke gevallen gelijk behandeld. Discriminatie wegens godsdienst, levensovertuiging, politieke gezindheid, ras, geslacht of op welke grond dan ook, is niet toegestaan." Section 1 of The Dutch Constitution since 1983.
4. For the parliamentary debates and the original proposals see: *Algehele Grondwetsherziening, eerste lezing, deel Ia, Grondrechten, Tweede Kamer* (General Revision of the Constitution, First Reading, Part Ia, Second Chamber); Den Haag: Staatsuitgeverij, 1979 (government publication with original texts).
5. Raad van State.
6. Section 26 of the International Covenant on Civil and Political Rights, New York, 1966.
7. "Onder het maken van onderscheid naar geslacht wordt mede verstaan het maken van onderscheid op grond van gedragingen of uitingen in strijd met aan het geslacht van de betrokkene(n) toegeschreven eigenschappen of kenmerken." *Advies over de Wenselijkheid van Een Wet Tegen seksediskriminatie* (Advice on the Desirability of an Act Against Sex Discrimination); Emancipatiekommissie, Rijswijk, 1977, p. 38.
8. For the U.S. see: Babcock, B. A. and others (1975) *Sex discrimination and the law*. Boston: Little, Brown. For the U.K., see: Pannick, D. (1983) Homosexuals, Transsexuals and the Sex Discrimination Act. In *Public Law*, Summer 1983, pp. 279-302.
9. "Eiseres is immers niet ontslagen op grond van een eigenschap, waarmee zij is behept, maar zij werd ontslagen op grond van daden of gedragingen harerzijds." Kantonrechter (local judge) Leeuwarden, 29-02-1972, *Nederlandse Jurisprudentie* (Dutch Law Reports) 1972, 356.
10. A list of 54 reported cases on homosexuality is included in: Waaldijk, K., *"Handelingen welke de indruk konden wekken van tederheden zoals die tussen geliefden plegen te worden gewisseld." Over de woorden die de rechter gebruikt om*

and youths, manuals for parents and other educators appeared as well (de Regt 1982).

Apparently, sexuality was becoming an important subject to read or write about. As for this, the high sales figures of many instruction books speak for themselves. It is the very massive way in which these books penetrated into Dutch living rooms, schools, and libraries which turned them into an important source of information and influence with regard to questions concerning sexuality in general, and to homosexuality in particular. In this article we shall focus on the latter aspect: What can sex-instruction books, which appeared in The Netherlands after 1940, tell about homosexuals and homosexuality?

METHODS

The primary questions raised in our research were:

1. Exactly what shifts have occurred in the information about homosexuality; what descriptions, arguments, and advice have been given and how did they change in the course of time?
2. How should we interpret and judge the changes that have occurred from a homosexual rights perspective?

We started our research by collecting instruction books for youths up to the age of 20 via libraries, mouth-to-mouth publicity, and a notice in the university newspaper at the University of Utrecht. In this way 71 books came into our possession. Of these 71 books, 16 have been published between 1940 and 1960, 18 between 1961 and 1970, and 37 between 1971 and 1982.

Each book was analyzed by one of the authors based on the questions listed below. In most cases, answering these questions proved not to pose any problems; if obscurity did exist after all, the four authors were able to come to a quick agreement through mutual consultation.

The questions addressed were: (a) in what way is homosexuality described; (b) what causes of homosexuality are mentioned; (c) how is homosexuality judged morally; (d) to what extent is the social oppression of homosexuals pointed out; (e) does the author directly address himself to the reader as a potential homosexual; (f) to what extent is sexual conduct between homosexuals described; (g) is information about the homosexual subculture being given; (h) is what ways are relationships between homosexuals described; and, (i) is a description of the personal process of acceptance of homosexuals being given.

Next we classed the books by 1 of the following 3 categories through mutual consultation. The norm for this classification was conforming to 2 or more of the above qualifications. (We realize that such a norm has an arbitrary character.)

Category 1: Rejecting Books

Among these were books about sex and relationships which either ignored homosexuality or which conformed to one or more of the following qualifications: (a) homosexuality is associated with seduction in one's youth; sin; a psychic aberration; criminality; seduction of children; (b) homosexuals are looked upon as people who need expert help; and (c) the relationship pattern of homosexuals is regarded as "below the mark."

Category 2: Accepting Books

This category included books that conformed to 2 or more of the following qualifications: (a) prejudices (as mentioned in the above category) are put right; (b) homosexuals are regarded as a socially oppressed group; (c) the writer directly addresses himself to the reader as a potential homosexual; (d) the interest and relief organizations pertaining to homosexuals are mentioned; and, (e) various sexual techniques are described.

Category 3

This constituted a middle category of books to which the qualifications of both the first and the second category applied, and which stood mid-way between rejecting and an accepting approach; for example, by discreetly calling for understanding for the problems of the homosexual.

The books examined were subdivided per category into the three aforesaid periods. Moreover, the frequency of each separate qualification was calculated per period. The data of these calculations are summarized in Tables 1 and 2.

REJECTING BOOKS

From our analysis, it appeared that over a period of years the percentage of rejecting books dropped from 94% between 1940-1960, via 56% in 1961-1970, to 32% in 1971-1982. This did not mean that all these books contained negative stories about homosexuality, for these percentages also included all books which do not mention homosexuality at all. Especially during the period 1940-1960, homosexuality did not appear to be

Table 1

Division of Categories of Instruction Books Over Three Periods (in %)

		40-60	61-70	71-80
Rejecting:	Homosexuality ignored	56	28	14
Rejecting:	Homosexuality is disapproved of	38	28	19
- Rejecting, totally		94	56	32
- Middle Category		6	33	19
- Accepting		0	11	49

Table 2

Division of Rejecting and Accepting Qualifications Over Three Periods (in %)

		1940-1960	1961-1970	1971-1982
	Homosexuality as a result of seduction in one's youth	29	46	19
Rejecting Qualifications	Homosexuality as a psychic abberation	57	23	28
	Homosexuality as a sin	14	0	3
	Homosexuality as a crime	14	0	3
	Homosexuality as seduction of children	29	8	0
	Homosexuality as an indication for expert help	29	46	9
	Homosexual relationship pattern below the mark	14	8	3
Accepting Qualifications	Social oppression of homosexuals being mentioned	29	38	66
	Book aimed at homosexual as a potential reader	0	15	28
	Interest groups and relief organizations pertaining to homosexuals are mentioned	0	8	34
	Homosexual conduct is being described	0	0	22
	Prejudices are put right	14	46	41

a subject in which sex, love, and relationships were in question. In the books of the 1960s and 1970s we noticed that this disregard was lessening. If we left the books in which homosexuality was ignored out of consideration, the shift in pronouncing adversely on homosexuality was: 38%-38%-19%.

A number of our qualifications appeared, more than others, to produce clear differences between the three periods. It can be noted that the theologically based books, in which homosexuality was regarded as a sinful error, especially marked the first period. As marriage was ''an explicit commandment of God'' (Drogendijk, 1949, p. 15), everything that was not directed toward marriage was condemned without more ado, particularly homosexuality. Fortunately, the Bible also pronounces upon this subject, so that J. van Gijs unblushingly thought he had to pour the following over his readers: ''The Bible clearly teaches us that God has a profound distaste for homosexuality which in our days raises its loathsome head more and more impudently and shamelessly'' (p. 108, p. 106). After 1960 such notions figured much less frequently in instruction books. Besides the preachers of sin, the medical/psychiatric model held an important place in the first period. ''From a materialistic point of view, the unnaturalness of homosexuality lies in the negation of a biological purpose. The objectionable lies in its spiritual sterility, which expresses itself in physical infertility and in the allied accentuation of sexual lust'' (Tolsma, 1948, p. 154). With much scientific verbosity homosexuality was shown to be not so much a sin as a psychic dysfunctioning as a result of a warped development of the personality. With the psychoanalysis in hand, scientists explained that in the development of a homosexual from child to adult, a hitch has occurred. The bossy mother, the weak or absent father, the unsolved Oedipus complex caused the child's inability to identify with a parent of the same sex. In over half (57%) of the instruction books from the 1940s to the 1960s this model was used. Although this percentage had been more than halved after 1960, the psychic disorder continued to play a role in instruction literature. Kahn and Heyermans (1968) wrote, ''But most experts look upon homosexuality as a neurosis, that is to say a disorder in character development which is deeply anchored in one's youth'' (p. 189). And Freud remarked that homosexuality is essentially a form of narcissism (Family Encyclopedia for Sexual Education, 1976).

A shift occurred from pointing out causes with the help of psychoanalysis to descriptions of a phase in the psychosexual development of children. The reader, whether male or female, was soothingly informed that every child goes through a homosexual phase, with the inherent homosexual games, but that this need not be a reason for panic; generally it would wear off of its own accord. It only became painful if one stayed in this phase. "But even the most broadminded educator should acknowledge that a danger lies in it, namely that one gets stuck in this stage of development. And that is not pleasant at all!" (J. van Keulen, 1962, p. 93).

The digging for causes, especially psychic ones, was connected with the increase in advice to call in expert help if one experienced homosexual feelings. The great faith in the good advice of experts was especially manifest in the 1960s, as indicated by the expansion of the network of relief institutions during that period. Although the success of therapy with homosexuals was doubted everywhere, e.g., "Unfortunately, the success of treatment of homosexuality is much slighter than with other forms of neurosis" (Kahn & Heyermans, 1968, p. 189), it could not do any harm to try. And similar advice still had not completely disappeared in the 1970s, as evidenced by the following quotations. "And can he do something about it? That seems to be very difficult but it makes a difference how soon somebody takes this problem to a psychiatrist. The sooner, the better" (v. der Land, p.70). "And even if you never get rid of it, it is useful anyhow to unburden you heart and to talk about it in detail. There are people enough with whom you can talk straight. They know your troubles themselves. So talk and ask questions honestly; most of it you know already. The rest you talk over honestly with your parents, with a priest or vicar, with the family doctor, or another friend who is older than you are" (Stolker, 1957, p. 57). Advice for pastoral help was usually not so much aimed at healing as rather at the support of a spiritual adviser when seeking a suitable way of living, preferably by total continence from sexual pleasures. (Yet one book, "I Am Not Like That Anymore,'' about the miraculous healing of a homosexual, did, in fact, appear in the 1970s.)

Seduction of youths by homosexuals has been the subject of much of the literature on homosexuality for years (29% in 1940-1960, 46% in 1960-1970). Thus Stolker (1957) wrote with regard to the cause of homosexuality: "How many bigger boys and men do not regret not having been warned by their parents in the past. Now they are confronted with the misery themselves: often they become just as deviant as the men whom they started with.'' Other authors did not regard seduction as a direct cause, but they did caution extensively against its dangers. Love of ease, weakness, and shyness could induce the seduced youth to stay on the wrong track and, even if he could find the right track again, he might be left with considerable emotional impairment, or at least be temporarily restrained from contacts with the other sex. And the horrible consequences it could have on conjugal bliss could easily be guessed. That the seducer, male or female, was usually depicted none too positively is self-evident. Thus we read in "When a Girl Becomes a Woman'' (Kent, 1963, p. 95), "The natural affectionateness and the need of love of the younger girl are, however, not infrequently misused by the older girl-friend as attempts to make physical advances. Of course, the young girl would not allow herself to be deterred in this by anything, not even by the entreaties of the old woman.'' Even after 1970, seduction was still being described in 19% of the books.

Although it was generally older men and women who were said to seduce youths to homosexual deeds, the link with paedophilia was not always automatically made. All the same, in over a quarter of the books that appeared between 1940-1960, a homosexual was identified with a child seducer; between 1961-1970 this percentage dropped to 8%, and after 1970 it was no longer mentioned.

Sometimes the law was dragged in and homosexuals were labeled criminals by the author, although this did not happen very often. It was, however, frequently mentioned that homosexuality with minors was included in the Penal code, which implicitly cited disapproval of such behavior.

If the relationship pattern of homosexuals was being described at all, it was in very divergent ways. Sometimes comparisons were made with heterosexual relationships in general and with marriage in particular, but if so as positive exceptions.

But the judgment "far below the mark" also resounded in the descriptions of the relationship pattern between homosexuals:

> Sometimes such a man finds a friend whom he starts living together with and sets up housekeeping with as if it were a question of a real marriage. But most of them keep seeking restlessly and occasionally have a little hurried, superficial adventure with a fellow-sufferer, whose name they hardly know. For this is so questionable in this little world. . . . affairs like these are indeed very paltry compared with the richness of a dawning love between an amorous boy and his girl! (v. Keulen, 1962, p. 96)

Such ideas about relationships were found less and less over the course of years in question. Nevertheless, as late as 1976, it was still maintained in the Family Encyclopedia for Sexual Education, which was sugared with pseudoscientific coating, "that the homosexual conduct does not represent a sexuality to us in which we can talk of relationships" (p. 159).

THE MIDDLE CATEGORY

Beginning in the second half of the 1960s and thereafter, more books appeared which we reckoned among the middle catgory. Their authors made well-intentioned attempts to refute various prejudices, rejected the view of homosexuality as a disease and in general, pleaded for more understanding for the fate that the homosexual had to bear. Their basic idea was that, in essence, society had to accept homosexuals in their being different, for it was difficult enough for them as it was, and being a homosexual was definitely not a desirable situation. Typical was the call for tolerance combined with a warning intended for youths not to be too curious.

> One thing, however, we should never do: condemn homosexuals. We cannot know how big their problems are. Only for the so-called hangers-on, for those who merely make homosexual love out of curiosity or sensation, we need not make amends. (Diekman, 1961, p. 157)

> Now it is being talked about in a straight and business-like manner, one also hears voices that glorify homosexuality, praise and recommend it as if everyone should have experienced it once. Such experiences should be looked at very critically and be seriously rejected. No more than it is permitted to regard being different as inferior, is it useful to present something that makes life more difficult as particularly attractive? (Goldstein, 1968, p. 125)

Time after time the ambivalent attitude recurred. On the one hand, homosexuals were allowed to be themselves; on the other hand, they were not allowed to indulge in their longings. On the one hand, it was said that boys who feel one another's genitals should not be respected the less for it, but on the other hand they were not to be envied, either. Homosexuals were entitled to their little place in the sun, but youths preferably should be kept out of that little place. Nor were homosexuals themselves allowed to transgress the borders of their own little area. "As long as they confine their erotic relations to members of the same kind and do not try to approach (heterosexuals) erotically, we do not have the right to pass judgment on their private lives" (Bovet, 1974, p. 55).

Consequently, homosexuals should stay in their own world. And heterosexuals in theirs. The latter appeared very nicely from modern biblical interpretations, according to which homosexuals were allowed to engage in homosexual conduct, but heterosexuals were not. Thus, God's wrath in the Sodom story would have been especially directed against heterosexual men, who would have had normal intercourse with their wives. "The men of Sodom want to have it both ways" (van Wijk, 1978, p. 53). Also with regard to the text in Romans 1:26 about the shameful lusts of unnatural intercourse, it was written: "Here, too, we are concerned with heterosexual people, men and women. It is not a matter of (homosexuals) who have never had any sexual contact with someone of the other sex" (Idem, p. 52). On the one side, room is created for homosexuals and increasingly claimed by themselves, but on the other side conditions are attached to it. Thus, it was advised that homosexuals should refrain from making advances to youths. In the middle category of books, too, the homosexual was repeatedly warned against as:

A playboy-like man who pays attentions to a boy and offers him a dream-environment for a couple of hours (house along the canals, whiskey, stereo, music, soft carpets, exciting pictures), after which he unobtrusively turns him into an intimate partner! (Berger & Richter, 1972, p. 36)

In the same book, a 28-year-old lesbian was put upon the stage who declared that many girls become lesbian out of curiosity.

She had *completely* accepted that she is a lesbian. All the same she would prefer a love-affair with a man. That is why she denies herself many an adventure with girls because she does not want to feel responsible if these girls will be permanently attracted by the same sex. (p. 41)

The characteristic equivocality of the books discussed herein also appears from the striking contradiction between, on the one hand, the commandment "do not judge and do not condemn" and, on the other hand, the pronouncing of implicit or explicit judgments by the author himself. For example:

There are noble characters who control themselves. There are others who limit themselves to one partner whom they remain faithful to all of their lives. Others again are untrustworthy seekers of lust, degenerates, or psychic invalids. (Peverelli, 1969, p. 5)

According to this line of thought, as "members of the same kind," homosexuals must associate with one another in as responsible a fashion as possible, backed up by a tolerant, noncondemnatory outside world, in which charitable clergymen, physicians, or psychologists hold themselves ready to offer help. And, as said, the nature of the help could differ widely: divine healing, healing by psychiatric help, help in the "development of non-sexual sides of life," support to make living with this aberration more endurable, and so on. But at the same time, homosexuality was also becoming the problem of the heterosexual majority, which clung to prejudices and was now being exhorted to more neighborly love toward homosexuals. Gradually, more information was being given, for "to know much about it fosters mildness with other young people and helps the ones concerned to find the right track and development of inner life in their circumstances" (Karreman, 1957, p. 84).

For those "concerned" the texts contained rays of hope; the conceptions which had prevailed so far were, although cautiously, being queried. New questions could be posed. Criticism became possible, no matter how vaguely and ambiguously it was formulated. For example, referring to Romans 1:26, Smedes (1977) wrote, "I have no reason at all to doubt that Paul was right. But I would wish indeed we knew better why homosexuality should be unnatural" (p. 47).

The 1980s marked the threshold of a new period, the time of the "liberated, joyful homosexual." Once more the tone in which sex-instruction books are written would change. Besides, books with rejecting ambivalent points of view are still being published. The old religious and psychiatric traditions die hard and could crop up again and again in the future.

ACCEPTING BOOKS

After 1970 the number of accepting books clearly increased; an increase in the average number of accepting qualifications applicable per book was noted. In instruction books homosexuals were more and more looked upon as a group oppressed by society. According to this view, problems around homosexuality did not spring from the individual nature of homosexuals, but should be imputed to the rejecting attitude of society. "Homosexuality is not a problem whatever. However, the society in which we live and in which certain sexual conducts have to be oppressed and ridiculed does constitute a problem" (Donkers, et al., 1980, p. 130).

It seems obvious that such a vision could be an important support for homosexual youths. As the acceptance of homosexuality increased, it also became possible to address the homosexual as a potential reader as such. "But some of you will indeed be homosexual. . . .That feeling of being different has probably been a first indication for you" (Barnes, 1972, p. 143). All the same, the imaginative faculty of various authors still left much to be desired; after 1970 only 28% regarded homosexuals as potential readers and also addressed them accordingly. Apparently, dealing abstractly with the difficult subject of homosexuality was a great deal easier than writing about it openly and directly. One positive point was that, to an ever larger extent, the addresses of interest groups and relief organizations for homosexuals were included in many of these books. In the old instruction books this was not the case, partly because these organizations did not exist as yet, or else had to carry out their work secretly and under an obscure name. In the newer books, however, they were referred to more and more frequently (34%).

"If you become aware of (homosexual) feelings in yourself and you find it very difficult, you can talk about it with someone, for example with someone of the COC" (Cousins, 1980, p. 42). It is striking that only "civilized" and generally accepted institutions like the COC and the Schorer Foundation were mentioned. Other aspects of the homosexual subculture, such as bars, saunas, and parks were not mentioned at all.

Instruction books published since 1970 gave increasingly concrete descriptions of sexual conduct, even including homosexual conduct. Such frankness was prompted, in part, by a change in thought on the purpose of sexuality. Gradually, sexuality was more and more looked upon as something pleasureable; thus, it became possible to write more and more openly about forms of sexuality which were not directed toward procreation. However, in spite of all such frankness, after 1970 still only 22% of the books examined showed that the author dared give expression to that openness. Refuting inaccuracies, negative statements, and so forth, was a major part of accepting books. In particular, the thesis that seduction is the cause of homosexuality was often disproved. In general, it appeared that, compared with the books of the middle category, the tone of the accepting books had become more and more assertive. "Do not let yourself be talked into 'illness'. In spite of the fact that your preference occurs, you are not ill or abnormal" (de Regt, 1976, p. 76).

Some texts went even further by advocating a fighting attitude for homosexuals.

Homosexuality was neither an illness nor an abnormality, but on the contrary, the starting point of a social fight. "Being lesbian is a rather conscious choice and implies a good deal more than making love with women. In a world that expects you to go through life with men, loving women and opting for women has far reaching consequences for your existence." "Being lesbian is a style of living," so wrote women of the COC (Holtrop & Sikkens, 1981, p. 136). A view often occurring in rejecting books, namely that the relationship pattern of homosexuals would be below the mark, was often repeated in accepting books. For example, it was pointed out that, similar to heterosexual ones, homosexual relationships sometimes are of long duration and sometimes of short duration. As the monogamous marriage became less of a standard, the authors of instruction books increasingly emphasized being oneself and honoring one's own feelings.

> How did you come to be a homosexual? Is something wrong? Such questions are, in fact nonsensical. You have your feelings and that should be the end of the matter. Nowadays, everybody says it is so wonderful to be yourself. Well, in that case, that also applies to people who have homosexual feelings. (Rutgersstichting, 1980, p. 15)

> You do not *need* to swallow all interfering factors without comment, you *may* very well claim time and room to be together with your (female/male) friend for once. You do not *need* to always let yourself be called a ridiculous poseur when you are in love! (de Regt, 1976, p. 74) (emphasis added).

Yet such "progressive" statements often retain a rather noncommittal character after all. Quite a number of authors confined themselves to sounding a few tolerant notes, without giving information about the various aspects of the homosexual world. In this context, it was significant that not even half of the books that appeared after 1970 could be classed as accepting according to our criteria.

DISCUSSION

In The Netherlands the moral views on homosexuality became considerably more permissive in the period after the Second World War. Comparing random surveys of the Dutch population taken in 1968 and 1981 revealed, among other things, that the tolerance of homosexuality had strongly increased after 1968. Whereas in 1968 75% of the Dutch still embraced a negative or condemnatory attitude toward homosexuals, in 1981 this percentage had dropped to 21% (Nieuwe Revue, December 1981). These data, which pointed toward a climate less harmful to homosexuals, were confirmed by the results of our research: The information in instruction books about homosexuality had clearly become more tolerant and, only incidently, books with discriminatory utterances had appeared on the market. Verhelst arrived at a similar conclusion after an analysis of 65 recent German and Dutch instruction books for youths published between 1970 and 1980 (Verhelst, 1981). We examined 29 of the 39 Dutch books analyzed by Verhelst. In 85% of these books homosexuality was considered allowable, and out of the 6 books Verhelst regarded as restrictive, 5 appeared in the period 1970-1974. It was particularly in the second half of the 1970s that permissiveness regarding masturbation, premarital relations, contraception, and abortion seemed to increase significantly. The old norms, predominantly determined by Roman Catholicism and Orthodox Protestantism, seemed to have lost their meaning to a significant extent.

All the same, this increased tolerance entailed its own restrictions and its dangers. As for the restrictions, we already pointed out that, according to our criteria, not even half of the books that appeared after 1970 could be called really accepting. Concrete descriptions of sexual conduct between homosexuals were mostly missing, the addresses of relief organizations were not always mentioned, and in general, the texts were written in a reserved manner. The same points were mentioned by Verhelst, who was of the opinion that most authors were quite non-committal and showed little willingness to be of assistance to youths in becoming aware of and accepting their homosexual feelings. Quite often they did not go beyond the reassuring remark that everybody goes through a homosexual phase. Indeed, the homosexual experiences of youths were rarely if ever discussed in print. Furthermore, topics such as the homosexual night life, the annual homosexual demonstration or, to mention something quite different, homosexual foster-parenthood, were seldom discussed. In short, the contents of these books were tolerant but not diverse.

When authors of instruction books and many other experts in the field of sexology attribute to homosexuals a specific place and identity, it is implied that homosexuals can be placed. In reality, however, the categorical characteristics of homosexuality seem to evolve along with those individuals the authors attempt to categorize.

From one perspective, the existence of the concept of homosexuality might have a liberating effect for many because it offers them a recognition of their own feelings, and because it presents them with possibilities for expressing those feelings. On the other hand, the concept of homosexuality does not signify anything but a non-individualistic category people can conform to.

According to Foucault, the openness in modern instruction books concerning homosexuality and the invitation to talk about it with people of the same age, with professionals in this field, or both, has arisen with the confession (Foucault, 1980). In older instruction books we still read, for example, "Advise the child to choose itself a confessor, whom it confides in" (Dufoyer, 1942, p. 47), and "Be always very open-hearted in the confessional stall and look upon the priest as your spiritual 'father' in reality" (Jansen, 1952, supplement "Motherhood and Fatherhood for Boys," p. 8). Whereas such talking about one's "own" sexuality is considered by modern authors to be, above all, a way toward acceptance of self and emancipation, in our opinion it could also be interpreted as an invitation to classify yourself within one of the existing, social frameworks. In that way the label "homosexuality" remains equivocal; it might effect a separation between those who are like that and those who are not. As a consequence, homosexuality will never be liberated because as soon as a society recognizes it, it will simultaneously attempt to categorize and normalize homosexuals.

Therefore, the recently published "progressive" instruction books deserve our attention as well because, unintentionally, they might contribute to the categorization and fixation of homosexuality, even if only by the special treatment of this subject in one chapter. When a certain tolerance toward homosexuals exists, as is presently the case in The Netherlands, it is necessary to remain critical of educational materials.

REFERENCES

A.J.A.H. (Amsterdamse Jongeren Aktiegroepen Homoseksualiteit). (1971). Jongen-jongen/meisje-meisje; Bert Bakker/N.V.S.H.
Barnes, K. C. (1972). Hij en zij; Veen, Wageningen.
Berger, R., & Richter, O. (1972). Eerste liefde, eerste sex; Becht, Amsterdam.
Bitoux le J., Duyves, M., & Le Gai Pied. (1982). Interviews met Foucault; De Woelrat, Boskoop/Utrecht.
Bovet, Th. (1974). Jij en ik; Zomer en Kennig, Wageningen.
Cousins, J. (1980). Veel plezier; Bert Bakker, Amsterdam.
Donkers, G., & Janssen, J., & Yssel H. V. D., (1980). Seks is meer . . . dan recht op en neer; Stichting Publikaties SOF, Nijmegen.
Donzelot, J. (1979). The policing of families; Pantheon, New York.
Drogendijk, A. C. (1949). Onze roeping in het onderscheid der geslachten; Kok, Kampen.
Dufoyer, P. (1942). Voorlichting van kinderen, beginselen en concrete formuleringen; De Fontein, Utrecht—Imprimatur.
Foucault, M. (1980). Scienta sexualis (Histoire de la sexualité—la volonté de savoir) in: Te elfder ùre, p. 174-192; Sun, Nijmegen.
Gezinsencyclopedie voor de sexuele voorlichting;
    (1974) deel 4; 14-16 jaar, Zuid Nederl. uitgeverij, Harderwijk.
    (1976) deel; volwassenen, Zuid Nederl. uitgeverij, Harderwijk.
Goldstein, M. (1968). Geen vlinderliefde; N.V.S.H., Den Haag.
Gijs van, J. (1960). Sexualiteit in het licht van de Bijbel; Gideon, Gorkum.
Holtrop, A., & Sikkes, R. (1981). Het meidenboek; SARA, Amsterdam.
Jansen, Anth. M. (mgr.) (1952). De praktijk van de voorlichting; St. Gregoriushuis, Utrecht—Impramatur Driebergen.
Kahn, F., & Heyermans, H. (1968). Het sexuele leven en de jonge mens; Bert Bakker, Amsterdam.
Karreman-Vermeer, H. (1957). Liefde begint bij 14; Engelhard v. Embden, Amsterdam.
Kent, E. (1963). Als een meisje vrouw wordt; Ruys, Amsterdam.
Keulen, van J. (1962). Jongens vragen; Oisterwijk, Den Haag.
Land, van der S. (1973). Hoe zit dat?; Kok, Kampen.
Meyer, R. (1981). Sexuele vorming in het onderwijs; doktoraalskriptie. Inst. voor Klinische psych. preventie en psychotherapie, Utrecht.

N.V.I.H.—C.O.C./Schorerstichting (1981). Ook zo?! Informatie voor jogeren over homoseksualiteit; Amsterdam.

Nijnatten, van C. (1982). De strijd van de verkeerde kant; Interne publikatie Inst. voor Ontwikkelingspsychologie, Utrecht.

Peverelli, P. (1969). Geen blad voor de mond; Agon Elsevier, Amsterdam.

Postma, C. (1965). Stippellijnen in het seksuele leven (voor jongens van 13-18 jaar); Callenbach, Nijkerk.

Regt, de W. (1976). Met sex moet je leren leven; Kosmos, Amsterdam/Antwerpen.

Regt, de W. (1982). Van verstandig ouderschap tot jurkangst. Geschiedenis van de seksuele voorlichting vanaf 1954 in: Orlando, nr. 2.

SKRIPT/tijdschrift voor geschiedenisstudenten (1982). Interview met Michel Foucault: 'mannenrelaties in historisch perspectief'; nr. 2.

Smedes, L. B. (1977). Ik man, ik vrouw, Kok, Kampen.

Stolker, P. J. (1957). Onbehangen voorlichting; de Toorts, Haarlem.

Tolsma, F. J. (1948). Homosexualiteit en homoerotiek; Daamen's, 's Gravenhage.

Verhelst, A. (1981). Leerboeken voor sexuele opvoeding, een kwantitatieve inhoudsanalyse; Interfacultair Instituut voor Familiale en Sexuologische wetenschappen, Katholieke Universiteit, Leuven.

Volkskrant, de: Amsterdam, 9-1-1983.

Wijk, van P. C. (1978). Jeugd en sexualiteit; hulp bij bijbelstudie; Buijten en Schipperheijn, Amsterdam.

Pedophilia and the Gay Movement

Theo Sandfort
University of Utrecht

ABSTRACT. A history of literature and views existing within the COC (Cultural and Recreational Center), the major Dutch organizations of homosexual men and women, regarding pedophilia and its relationship to homosexuality are discussed, beginning with definite separation between the pedophile and homosexual identities and ending with an abolishment of oppression towards pedophilia, for which the COC is in part responsible. The article argues that the homosexual identity is by no means a "constant" but a fluid identity, based on societal views and conditions. By accepting pedophilia, the COC hopefully will broaden the idea of the gay identity.

Homosexuality and pedophilia are relatively incompatible social phenomena. In the Netherlands homosexuals and pedophiles are organized in separate movements with divergent goals, and the gay movement in particular has often been negative in its attitudes toward pedophilia and pedophiles.[1]

Despite this long-standing antipathy, in 1980 the most important organization of homosexual men and women in the Netherlands, the Cultural and Recreational Center (COC),[2] adopted the position that the liberation of pedophilia must be viewed as a gay issue. In order to trace the development of the COC's attitude toward pedophilia,[3] a content analysis was carried out on the vari-

Theo Sandfort is a Research Associate at the Department of Clinical Psychology at the State University of Utrecht. The author would like to thank Walter Everaerd and Lex van Naerssen for their comments on an earlier version of this article, and Michael Dallas for the translation of the article. Reprint requests may be addressed to the author, Department of Clinical Psychology, State University Utrecht, P.O. Box 80140, 3508 TC Utrecht, The Netherlands.

© 1987 by The Haworth Press, Inc. All rights reserved.

ous periodicals published by this organization from its founding in 1946 until 1981.[4]

Based on the findings of this study, the post World War II years can be roughly divided into 4 periods, although it must be noted that both positive and negative views were being voiced in all periods. In the first period, 1946-1958, pedophilia cannot be said to have existed as a category independent of homosexuality; and pedophiles, although controversial at times, constituted an important part of the COC. The second period, 1959-1963, was marked by growing estrangement between homosexuality and pedophilia; the two came to be viewed as separate categories, a development which appears to have been influenced largely by the aspirations of homosexuals for societal acceptance. Following a virtual purge of pedophile elements from the organization, a third period, 1964-1974, ensued, characterized by vehement rejection of pedophilia by the COC. And finally, in a fourth period from 1975 to the mid-1980s, pedophilia received increasingly positive attention, which resulted in an official policy statement by the COC calling for the liberation of child sexuality and pedophilia.

THE PAEDOPHILE[5] AND OTHER HOMOSEXUALS, 1946-1958

The early magazines of the COC were frequently embellished with illustrations of young boys. Numerous photographs and reproductions of paintings or sculptures showed youths in varying poses, naked or clothed, their facial hair and sometimes even pubic hair absent. The pictures were suggestively romantic and altogether unrealistic. Sexual behavior was almost never hinted at openly, but this was also true of illustrations involving adults. Only rarely could a picture be found showing a naked man and a naked boy together. After 1955, pictures of boys appeared with decreasing frequency.

Illustrations such as these sometimes stood alone, as on the magazine cover; more often, however, they accompanied stories or poems in which boys played a leading role. Poems by well-known Dutch poets such as Jacob Israël de Haan, Louis Couperus, and Willem de Mérode were printed, poems which often bore such suggestive titles as "Sleeping Youth," "Dying Youth," "Business Boy," and "Portrait of a Florentine Youth." In many poems, the puerile body was glorified and the poet's own desires toward the boy sung, although almost always platonically. In a rare poem sexual desires also played a role.

Boys were also a frequent subject of published short stories and novel excerpts, as well as of books reviewed in the magazine. Eroticism, both between boys themselves and between boys and older men, formed an important theme. Sometimes it was clearly sensual, but seldom was it openly sexual. Stories were often set in other times or other cultures, as was revealed by titles such as "Michelangelo's Young Friends" and "Arabian Nights." During 1946 a series of articles by Arent van Santhorst[6] was published about homo-erotic elements in boys' books.

The French writers André Gide and Roger Peyrefitte, referred to as "kindred spirits," received regular attention, with particular emphasis on their devotion to youths. The pedo-erotic novels *Costa Brava* and *Vervolgde minderheid* (Persecuted Minority) by the Dutch writer Servatius[7] which portrayed amorous relationships between men and boys of 12 and 15 years of age, were also reviewed. These as well as other books on paedophile homosexuality were proclaimed as books "in our domain" and were frequently promoted. The fact that they were available through the COC, however, evoked protests from some readers.

Considerable attention during this initial period was also devoted to "Greek Love." Stories set in Greek and Roman times, such as the legend of the Greek boy Antinous, lover of the Roman emperor Hadrian, appeared regularly. There was a review of Plato's *Symposium,* as well as of a book on Ovid that depicted how Orpheus taught the men of Thrace the art of loving boys, showing them "that such love affairs will revive the strength of their younger years, the innocence of youth, and the flowers of spring."

Various attempts were made to arrive at a clear description of the essence of Greek Love, or "paedophilia," but these yielded contradictory results. At first, paedophilia was viewed as an escape from the overwhelming polarity of the male-female relationship. Later, however, paedophilia became the pursuit of the very polarity inherent in the age difference between a man and a boy. At other times, the chief emphasis was placed on the platonic nature of paedophile relationships. "Sacred paedophilia," it was warned, should in no way be confused with "profane pederasty," the former being concerned not only with the beauty of the youth's body but also with that of his soul. Such contradictions suggested that the purpose of these essays was not so much to describe Greek Love objectively as to create an idealistic image of it.

Additional contributions discussed how the homosexual should conduct himself toward his "young friend," especially stressing his enormous responsibility. "If he is aware that the boy does not have a homo-erotic disposition—and this will quickly be evident—then he must under no circumstances try to reshape him in that direction." Moreover, "the knowledge that relationships with youths are so transitory should not entice him into such a frenzy that he starts up an intimate relationship with a new boy every day."

Paedophiles were clearly considered an important group among homosexuals during these years 1946 to 1958. It was argued that the manifestations of homosexual friendship extended from "the paedophile relationship to lasting (permanent) cohabitation by two partners"; marriage, therefore, did not constitute an adequate model for "our relationships." In articles dealing with the treatment of pedophile offenders by probation officers, men who sought sexual contact with boys younger than 16 were often, though not consistently, referred to as "homosexuals.'' Some writers spoke of the important role that "paedo-philes gifted with leadership abilities" played in the COC.

Seldom did an article define more specifically what was understood by the term "a homosexual." One such attempt was made in 1949 by one of the founders of the COC. He pointed out that three more or less related groups of homosexuals could be distinguished: inverts, paedophiles, and normal homosexuals. Inverts were seen as a biological variation; they were completely feminine and passive, often bearing female nicknames and occupying female professions. Their ideal was the *real* man. The ideal of the paedophiles, or "homo-eroticists, homo-idealists, or platonists," was centered on the youthfulness and the physical appearance of the love object. Sexuality was not their most prominent concern, however. As born pedagogues, they found gratification in the fruits of their educational efforts rather than in the reciprocal love of the child. "Normal homosexuals" were "neither avowed inverts, nor avowed paedophiles." Their relationships with lovers were based on faithfulness and love rather than on age or appearance. Because paedophiles were, of the three types, the most immune to women, they would therefore come closest to being true homosexuals.

The diversity of interest in boys revealed by the COC magazines in this period could not be called objective, for one of its functions was obvious: to titillate the erotic desires of the adult male homosexual readers.[8] It would seem plausible to conclude that the homosexual identity manifesting itself in these magazines during the 1950s was so broad or so undefined that it by no means excluded erotic feelings toward boys. In any case, within the male membership of the organization erotic desires seemed to be present not only for other men of the same age but also for boys of significantly younger age. Within the COC at this time, these paedophiles were viewed not as a separate category of persons, but first and foremost as homosexuals; this was evident, for example, in the above-mentioned scheme classifying different types of homosexuals. Until the late 1950s no assertions apparently were made in the magazines suggesting that paedo-philia might be a social entity independent of homosexuality.

Nonetheless, the presence of paedophile homosexuals within the COC was not taken for granted by all members. From the very beginning, disparaging voices could also be heard. A notice appearing in 1949, for example, called upon members to "pro-tect and refrain from harassing the immature youth."[9] Such neg-ative attitudes were becoming stronger toward the end of the pe-riod, and could be seen as an attempt by some homosexuals to distance themselves from paedophile homosexuality.

One 1954 article distinguished two forms of "homophilia": "paedophile" and "mixed" homophilia. The former pertains to "affection towards the inwardly immature on the part of persons deeming themselves more mature," whereas the latter form con-cerns "love which essentially seeks a closeness rooted in equal-ity." Compared to the scheme discussed above, here the paedo-phile was judged more negatively, indeed almost as pathological. The element "youth" was said to figure more prominently in the infatuations of the paedophile than the element "the right per-son." He refused to recognize the femininity in himself and was consequently incapable of relating to women in any way. "Dur-ing the homo-erotic phase, he became fixated on comradely love, so that the boy now fulfills for him, as it were, the role of the girl, supported in part by a male-worshipping society." The author went on to advocate a society in which paedophiles could "move on into relations more human than are possible with young people."

During the period 1946 to 1958, there was a growing tenden-cy to pathologize paedophilia, while at the same time attempts by outsiders similarly to pathologize the likewise deviant peer-oriented homosexual preference were being strongly resisted. Paedophilia was described by some writers as a perversion and a form of homosexuality founded in a developmental disorder. Some warned against the danger of "latent and unconscious homosexuals in the youth movement, in schools, and in scouting.'' Similar contentions were being voiced by many mental health authorities, who beginning in early 1960s campaigned outside the COC for the acceptance of homosexuality between consenting adults.

Speculations over the numerical relationships between the various kinds of sexual preferences drew varying conclusions. One article, for instance, asserted that paedophilia referred to a love relationship between an adult and a child, ''and this is usually a homosexual relationship.'' Other articles, however, noted that it had by no means been proven ''that the frequency of love for the young (paedophilia) is greater among homosexuals than among heterophiles.'' The ''misconception that all homosexuals should be attracted to the youthful or the pubescent'' was brought about by a small number of homosexuals who achieved notoriety by breaking the law, thereby coming into contact with social workers. It's obvious that speculations such as these were based on strategic considerations. The assumption was implicit that, should there prove to be just as much heterosexual as homosexual pedophilia, then homosexuals did not need to account for homosexual pedophilia in any special way.

Both the positive and the negative attention given paedophile homosexuality in the COC magazine provoked heated reactions, and this apparently became a trying problem for the editors. In a postscript following one such reaction in 1958, they announced their decision to close, ''at least for the time being, this interesting debate on such a subject about which so little is known.''

THE SEVERANCE OF PEDOPHILIA FROM HOMOSEXUALITY, 1959-1963

One year after announcing an end to its publication of articles on paedophilia, the COC magazine commenced publication of a whole new series of articles on pedophilia by Brunoz.[10] From that point on, the older Dutch spelling ''paedophilie'' was replaced by the more modern form "pedofilie."[11] "Pedofilie" was presented in this series as the "most normal deviation," being located somewhere between the heterosexual norm and the homosexual deviation from that norm. According to these articles what captivated the pedophile was "smooth, hairless skin, gentle curvatures, freshness, the slender figure, ruddy cheeks, etc." The "true homophile, the typical man-loving male" would never be attracted to such a boyish image. The articles by Brunoz were later collected and brought out by the COC in pamphlet form.

As would be expected, the articles evoked numerous protests from readers, and it was found particularly objectionable that the COC should publish such a brochure, for it fostered the prejudice that homosexuals were pedophiles. Sex contacts between young persons and adults were considered excesses, and pedophiles should restrain themselves "heroically" in their sexual behavior. When the editors persisted in defending the publication, one reader wrote that the COC was an organization "of and for homosexuals, and there cannot and must not be room within it for other deviant lifestyles."

The series by Brunoz was interesting in that pedophilia was apparently viewed as a phenomenon largely independent of homosexuality and, at most, only loosely related to it. This was probably a reflection of the situation within the COC, where by this time pedophiles had come to be more and more isolated as a result of the negative attention they had received. Pedophile homosexuals stood in the way of societal acceptance of homosexuality because they confirm the bias that homosexuals seduced children. On the other hand, the rift appeared also to have been induced by the isolated pedophiles themselves as a strategical measure. An alternative notion of pedophilia, independent of homosexuality, was constructed, which resulted in two separate categories of people. Only in this manner could pedophiles retain a positive self-image. In addition, by this time it had become possible to build a pedophile liberation movement outside the realm of the COC, an organization in which there seemed to be no place for pedophiles in the future.

A further indication that pedophilia and homosexuality were being increasingly defined as separate and independent categories could be found in the preliminary announcement for a symposium to be held in 1960 by the International Committee for Sexual Equality.[12] The theme of the symposium was to be "Pedophilia versus homosexuality," and the distinction between the two concepts was thoroughly elaborated in the accompanying commentary. In the end, for reasons which remained unclear, the symposium was not held. Articles appearing in the COC magazine around this time reinforced the distinction, arguing that "the psychologies of these differing types must also be very different."

One of the foremost issues in the early Dutch homosexual civil rights movement was the campaign for the repeal of Article 248-bis of the Netherlands Penal Code.[13] Under this Article homosexual contacts between adults and young people from 16 to 21 years of age were a criminal offense. Simultaneously with the emergence of the distinction between pedophilia and homosexuality, the argumentation for the repeal of Article 248-bis was also transformed. Initially it had been argued that the article discriminated against homosexuals, and particularly against the pedophiles among them. The Article was considered to measure by two standards because heterosexual adults were permitted to have sex with young persons 16 years of age and older. Later however, the campaign increasingly came to center around the argument that the Article impeded the development of young homosexuals by forcing them into sexual abstention.

During the 1960s, the COC became more active in providing assistance and support to young homosexuals, a policy which met with a good deal of opposition from many within the organization, on the grounds that it might increase the temptation for some members to break the law, thereby giving the COC a bad name. It was not until 1970, one year before the repeal of

248-bis, that young people 16 years and older were permitted to become members. The decision to allow this was defended by the COC as follows: Adult homosexuals no longer need to be protected from temptation, for they are old and wise enough to resist it on their own.

DISSOCIATION FROM PEDOPHILIA AND OTHER NONCONFORMIST HOMOSEXUAL BEHAVIOR, 1964-1974

Around 1964 an important policy change took place within the COC, marked by increased emphasis on gaining societal acceptance of homosexuality. The magazine of the organization implemented this change, linking up to current developments in society and giving more attention to homosexual women. At the same time, two persons who had regularly written about pedophilia disappeared from the editorial staff without explanation.

The divorce of homosexuality from pedophilia was virtually complete by this time within the COC, but two important prejudices pertaining to homosexuality still lived on in society: it was still believed that homosexuals seduce young people and that through this seduction young people become homosexuals.

The COC magazine waged a constant campaign from many angles against the idea that young people become homosexual by seduction. When the seduction theory is once again propagated in its pages by an external "expert" in 1966,[14] the editors distanced themselves from this standpoint in a subsequent issue.

The dangers posed by seduction played a prominent role in the adoption of Article 248-bis in 1911, but in the sixties a national advisory council report[15] advocating the repeal of the article expressed considerable doubts as to the validity of the seduction theory: "If a young person who has experienced a homosexual approach later proves to be a homosexual, it must be assumed that this person was already emotionally amenable to such an approach and had, as it were, been waiting for it to occur. The experience merely exerts a shaping influence on an existing homosexual orientation."[16] Certain cases of successful seduction, according to the report, did not lead to permanent homosexual identification, whereas in other cases young people reacted to an approach with a flat refusal, sometimes accompanied by either violence or a friendly admonition. The COC magazine quoted approvingly from this official report. After the repeal of Article 248-bis in 1971, the theme of seduction temporarily disappeared from the limelight, only to resurface in the late 1970s as a result of the much-publicized anti-gay campaign in the United States led by Anita Bryant.

With the effective elimination of pedophiles within the ranks of the COC, it became easier to counteract the prejudice that homosexuals seduced young people, especially as it existed within the educational system. Whenever homosexual teachers were fired or refused posts in schools, protests in the COC magazine were rife and were consistently accompanied by assurances that homosexual teachers had no sexual feelings towards young boys. After all, heterosexual teachers wouldn't harbor such feelings either. It was unclear, however, whether teachers indeed did not experience such feelings, or whether they did not allow themselves to experience them because of pressure from both society in general and from the homosexual movement. One teacher all but admitted these feelings in a special issue of the magazine on homosexuality and teaching when he wrote that he knew the names of all the boys in his class, but not of all the girls. "Because they are often intellectually as well as physically well-stocked, it is usually the boys that write on my blackboards."' The position of homosexuals in the teaching profession was an issue that received continual attention. In addition, lectures and newspaper reports suggesting that homosexuals seduce young people were publicized and repudiated as "affirming prejudice," and any association of homosexuality with criminality was indignantly disclaimed.

In contrast, the editors took no stand against comparable lectures and articles over pedophilia and pedosexuality in the period between 1964 and 1974. Some negative news reports were quoted without comment, which suggested editorial endorsement, and approval was likewise given to a portrayal of pedophiles as "sexually disturbed persons, who in putting their disturbed inclinations into practice ruin others for life." Pedophiles were people who tampered with young children. Warnings against child-molesters were cited: "Keep an eye on the friends of your 10-year-old son. . . . And never trust the youth leader or athletic instructor who wants to take him jogging in the woods or give him extra football training on his own." Sexuality with minors was rejected by the COC as absolutely unacceptable. In reply to a reader who asked whether the COC could not do something about the crimes of vice that threatened to destroy the hard-won goodwill toward homosexuals, the editors replied that it went without saying "that we also gag from murderers and men who molest children, whether they are office clerks who abuse little boys or schoolteachers who do it with little girls."

Informative articles on homosexuality published in this period emphasized strongly the distinction between it and pedophilia. Pedophiles "actually feel more comfortable with a woman than an (adult) male lover." Their coveted ideal was always marriage and not homophile friendship. "This again points out that there are essential differences between pedophiles and homosexuals." The clear distinction between homosexuals and pedophiles that supposedly came to light in Schofield's book[17] on the sociological aspects of homosexuality was referred to as a "remarkable discovery."

The dissociation of homosexuality from homosexual pedophilia cannot be viewed independently of the striving among many homosexuals in the 1960s to be seen as normal. In this drive to win societal acceptance, the homosexual identity most often put forward was that of the "well-adjusted homosexual differing from others only in choice of partner."[18] In addition, a campaign was waged against expressions of homosexuality which deviated from this image, such as camp and leather. Cross-dressing was warned against ostensibly because of local ordinances forbidding it and butch behavior became taboo for lesbians.[19]

In the late 1960s, spurred by feminism and student protests, the gay movement broadened its scope. The COC, however, still continued to propagate the image of the conventional homosexual desiring a lasting relationship with a partner of the same age. Within the context of the sexual revolution, attention was given in the magazine to other forms of sexuality such as transvestitism and incest, but this met with considerable disfavor among readers. A survey revealed great differences of opinion "over articles that have little or nothing to do with homosexuality, but which do manifestly break other taboos." Criticism of established structures was nevertheless stepped up and extended to areas other than sexuality. One result of this increased social consciousness was the COC's endorsement of certain political parties in the 1972 elections. Although expressly not intending to concern itself with everything, the COC called for solidarity with others who deviated from the norm. Its policies aimed at a "genuinely integrated, diversified society." In this context attention was also given to the position of young people, and a new conception of child sexuality was advocated, one which proposed that not only gays and straights, women and men, but also children and adults, including parents, should have equal rights and social status. The COC policy statement for 1974 criticized the patronizing of children; authoritarian structures both in the family and in school should be replaced by democratic practices. Such concern with child-rearing was at no time stronger in the COC magazine than it was in the early 1970s.

With regard to pedophilia, the meaning of this interest in youth emancipation remained unclear. Editorials toward the end of this period insisted that the COC did not conform to existing prejudices toward pedophilia, pointing out that child molestation and pedophilia could not be considered as one and the same thing. Yet the editors continued to view pedophilia as a problem, arguing that by their nature pedophile relationships were based on dependency. In 1974 the editors announced that a special publication would be devoted to relationships of dependency, but such never appeared.

All in all it was clear that pedophilia was not seen as an alternative of equal merit to homosexuality. The editors continued to deny any assertion suggesting a link between homosexuality and pedophilia, insisting that pedophilia was an unconnected phenomenon and pointing out that pedophiles could also be heterosexual or bisexual. A major confrontation over the subject took place in 1974 following a nationwide broadcast on sexuality between children and adults aired by one of the two Dutch television networks. In this program pedophiles were interviewed who two years earlier had formed their own pressure group outside the COC, under the auspices of The Netherlands Society for Sexual Reform (NVSH).[20] According to the COC, the program treated the question one-sidedly in favor of the interests of pedophiles, virtually ignoring the dependent position of children in relation to adults. The COC was also "extremely critical" of the fact that only relationships between men and boys were discussed in the program, thereby implying a connection between pedophilia and homosexuality. The existence of female and heterosexual pedophiles was overlooked. Furthermore, the pedophile group was upbraided for lacking a critical view of society. The COC protested to the NVSH, accusing that organization of "placing reflection over such delicate human relationships into the hands of persons unqualified for the task."

The reaction of the COC disregarded the fact that this incipient movement of pedophiles was still cautiously coming out of the bushes,[21] and was so to speak, in an infantile stage of development in contrast to the COC. It was therefore not surprising that the NVSH did not yet possess a broadly-founded viewpoint on pedophilia. The COC likewise failed to recognize in its criticism that the pedophile group consisted mainly of men with a homosexual preference.

TOWARD SOLIDARITY WITH CHILDREN AND PEDOPHILES, 1975-1981

In the course of the 1970s, nevertheless various signs became visible which suggested an increasingly favorable attitude toward pedophilia within the COC. Announcements of lectures on the subject organized by the NVSH cropped up regularly in the calendar of events for local COC chapters. A consciousness-raising group as well as consultation services for pedophiles were advertised. Books on pedophilia and youth sexuality were cited more frequently, and when reviewed by the COC they received positive critiques. Convictions resulting from consenting pedosexual contacts were criticized, and a favorable review was published of an NVSH report recommending the abolition of ages of consent for sex. Attention was given to prosecutions of foreign newspapers such as *Gay News* and *The Body Politic* for publishing articles on pedophilia, and to an article in a Dutch paper criticizing biases toward it.

In 1977 the COC produced a special issue on pedophilia which contained a non-judgmental portrayal of a man-boy love affair, as well as articles on pedophile women and police attitudes toward pedophilia. In yet another article, the COC's own attitude was criticized: "Undoubtedly, many homosexuals have been inclined to pass the Old Maid of discrimination on to the pedophiles."[22] In fact, however, the article went on, pedophiles were subjected to the same sort of discrimination as homosexuals. "A general human trait, diffused in greater or lesser proportions through the whole of society, is universally suppressed and ascribed only to one small group. This group becomes earmarked by that single trait, whereas sexual preference is only one aspect of a person, just like height, sex, left-handedness, skin color, and so on.''²² The writer argued that the COC could be a good deal more active toward combating the intense discrimination against pedophiles. He expressed the hope ''that we will once see the day when people will make no more of a fuss about pedophilia than they now do about left-handedness, birth-control devices, or the danger of getting spinal consumption by masturbation.''²²

The COC's growing amicability toward pedophilia appeared to have been stimulated to a great extent by the self-organization of pedophiles and their subsequent emergence into the public eye, which was in turn facilitated by the fact that sexual liberation during this period was generally considered an important societal value. After the distinction between heterosexual and homosexuals regarding age of consent had been eliminated in 1971, the age limit itself came under attack by pedophiles and other groups, and the resulting debate was carried on not only within organizations like the NVSH and the COC, but also in wider circles.

An additional factor prompting the COC's more favorable treatment of pedophilia was the increased opposition among gays to the conformist homosexual-idea of the 1960s. The practice of cultivating public sympathy and understanding for the fellow man or woman ''who happens to be gay'' became tantamount to the denigration of gays. The idea of self-acceptance was transformed into an imperative to come out into the open, confronting society with gay lifestyles.¹⁸ Radical gay groups outside the COC formed the vanguard in this change of strategy, but the COC gradually followed their example in the course of the 1970s. The principal concern lay in individuals opting for a gay identity, determining for themselves ''what'' they are, and shaping their own homosexuality, instead of trying to live up to the expectations of society. This viewpoint created room for other sexual forms such as pedophilia, transvestitism, and sadomasochism, which the gay movement had, for opportunistic reasons, formerly disdained.

However, this increased support for pedophilia provoked denouncement from thus far unexpected circles—including lesbian feminists. "In a society that sees women as the possession of men," they wrote, "nothing is more exciting than to possess an object that has never before been possessed." This attack formed one of the few instances in the late 1970s in which negative voices were heard within the COC regarding pedophilia.

As a result of the changing attitudes toward pedophilia, in 1980 the COC convoked a nation-wide conference for the purpose of working out a preliminary position on pedophilia to be voted on by the annual congress of the organization.[23] Adopting a position had become necessary, in part, because of discussions over the issue within the International Gay Association. In the circular announcing the conference, it was pointed out that the debate over pedophilia had long been held off by the COC. The organization's earlier stance condemning pedophilia was criticized, although it was conceded that that position had probably facilitated increased acceptance of homosexuality by society.

Criticism of the "moral code of compulsory heterosexuality" played an important role in the discussions during the conference. The dominant social code allowed for only one form of sexuality: between one man and one woman, lifelong, within a narrowly circumscribed role division based on male power. Both child-rearing methods and the education system were held responsible for sustaining heterosexual morality, which enforced the oppression of homosexuality, pedophilia, and child sexuality. On the basis of this analysis, the COC congress later resolved that "the struggle for the liberation of gay men and women (must) also strive for a radical change in notions regarding the sexuality of children and sexual relations between minors and adults. . . . Successful gay liberation must include pedo-liberation, or we will have achieved nothing."

The congress further held that mutually consenting contacts between children and adults were not harmful for those concerned. Any damage that did occur "results exclusively from existing societal condemnation of such contacts, which finds expression not only in the attitudes of parents and other persons responsible for children, but above all in the continuing liability to prosecution and the resulting interrogations and other procedures, convictions, and the fear of them.'' According to the congress ages of consent should therefore be abolished. On the other hand, protection should be afforded to children and adults alike against sexual violence, both mental and physical. Violence and other constraints should be deterred, not sexuality. In addition to adopting these standpoints, the congress also resolved to participate in activities directed at the revision of public morality legislation, to integrate these standpoints into its educational and publicity activities, and to support the development of informative materials on pedophilia and child sexuality.

CONCLUSION:
TOWARD A NEW GAY IDENTITY?

The future will have to tell whether the COC, by assuming standpoints like those of 1980, as a gay organization can contribute to ending oppression of pedophilia, an oppression which the COC itself has partly helped to foster. But this change of course could moreover have implications for homosexuals themselves. When the first COC magazine appeared in 1946, few models existed for people to identify with when becoming aware of their homosexual desires. The COC magazine provided a positive image of homosexuality, and this presumably played a determining role for the readers in learning to shape their homosexual desires and in acquiring a homosexual identity. As this article has attempted to show, that homosexual identity is far from a historical constant; rather, its content is dependent on societal conditions and is also influenced by the gay movement. Due to the growing visibility of homosexuality, such identification models for persons with homosexual feelings have meanwhile considerably increased, both in number and availability. Consequently, the role of COC publications in helping homosexuals form their personal identities has probably diminished. Nevertheless, by acknowledging the affinity between homosexuality and pedophilia, the COC has quite possibly made it easier for homosexual adults to become more sensitive to erotic desires of younger members of their sex, thereby broadening gay identity.

NOTES

1. Negative reactions from the gay movement have not been confined to the Netherlands, but are also commonplace in other countries such as Great Britain and the United States. See for example Reeves, T. (1983, June). "Man-Boy Scenes in the United States," Paper presented at the conference *Among Men, Among Women*, University of Amsterdam. In addition to portraying his own process of coming out as a boy lover, Reeves described in this paper the founding of the North American Man-Boy Love Association, NAMBLA, and the negative reactions to it from the left and from gay organizations. The international journal for man-boy love, *PAN*, which is published in the Netherlands, regularly reports on clashes between gay groups and pedophiles in countries throughout the world.

2. See Tielman, R., "The Dutch gay emancipation movement," elsewhere in this issue.

3. The spelling, and more importantly, the meaning of the concept pedophilia did not remain consistent during the period studied. Initially, for example, the term referred only to sexuality and, in particular, to love between men and boys, heterosexual and lesbian pedophilia did not seem to exist. Although it is not the intention of this article to trace the history of the concept of pedophilia, differences in meaning will sometimes be pointed out or will become evident in certain contexts. As will be made clear, the variations in intended meaning originated in part due to political considerations. One major change occurred with respect to the maximum age of the younger partner, which determined whether relationships were considered pedophile. In the Dutch literature on pedophilia, the maximum age employed at this writing is 15 years, on the grounds that only sexual contacts with persons 15 and younger are punishable by law. The research materials used for this article revealed, however, that in the 1940s and 1950s sexual attraction to boys of older age was also referred to as pedophilia. When pedophilia referred to older boys the term "ephebophilia" was also sporadically used. The lowering of the age limit was presumably influenced by the decriminalization in 1971 of homosexual contacts between adults and persons 16 years and older. (Cf. Salden, M. The Dutch penal law and homosexual conduct, elsewhere in this issue.)

4. Since its founding, the COC has published periodicals with varying titles; in some periods two periodicals were published simultaneously, one aiming at the members only, and the other at a wider audience. At all times, however, the number of copies printed slightly outnumbered the number of COC-members at the time (Tielman, R., personal correspondence).

DIRECTORY OF COC PERIODICALS

Title	Target Group	Period	Frequency
Levensrecht (Right to Live)	Members	1946-49	Approx. Monthly
Vriendschap (Friendship)	Members	1949-64	Monthly
Dialoog (Dialogue)	Members and Other Interested Parties	1965-68	Bi-monthly
De Schakel (The Link)	Members	1965-67	Monthly
De Schakelkrant (The Link Newsletter)	Members	1967-69	Monthly
Informatie Bulletin Dialoog	Members and Other Interested Parties	1968-72	Bi-monthly
Seq	Members	1969-71	Monthly
Sik	Active Members	1970-71	Approx. Monthly
Sec	Members	1971-73	Every 4 Weeks
Sek	Members and Other Interested Parties	1973-Present	Every 4 Weeks

All issues of these periodicals through 1980 were used for the content analysis. Publications of local chapters, as well as other potentially fruitful sources such as minutes of meetings, had to be omitted from the study for practical reasons. In the material, relevant texts were sought by means of catchwords and phrases such as *pedophilia, pedophile, children, boy, youth, youngster, young people, girl, child, sexuality, emancipation,* and *definition of homosexuality.* Illustrations were also observed. All quotations cited in this article are derived from periodicals listed above.

5. The use of the more traditional spellings "paedophilia" and "paedophile" in this section reflects comparable Dutch usage in the early publications. In these, the archaic Dutch spellings *paedophilie* and *paedophiel* are consistently maintained instead of the now standard spellings *pedofilie* and *pedofiel*, hinting that pedophilia is a practice rooted in classical antiquity. The corresponding English spellings are used here, where appropriate.

6. Arent van Santhorst was the pseudonym used by Jaap van Leeuwen, one of the founders of the COC. Until the early 1960s most people writing in the COC publications did so under pseudonyms.

7. Servatius was the pseudonym of Frits Bernard, an internationally known psychologist. *Costa Brava* was published in English translation in *Gay Sunshine Journal,*

no. 47 (1982). *Vervolgde minderheid* has been published in German under the title *Verfolgte Minderheit* by Foerster-Verlag, Berlin.

8. The titillation did not, however, occur openly, but was camouflaged and legitimized by transposing the actions to other eras or other cultures and by packaging it artistically. The illustrations must be viewed in the context of the immediate post-World War II period, when the depiction of nudity and sexuality in publications was taboo. But the editors undoubtedly practiced self-censorship as well. Initially, the activities and publications of the fledgling COC were closely shadowed by the police. Tamboer, K. (1972). "Justitiedossier." *Dialoog*, 1:1. The series referred to here about homo-erotic elements in boys-books had to be discontinued following objections by the public prosecutor.

Precisely which things are experienced as erotically exciting are greatly dependent on when and where they are published. The attention given to young boys in the early COC publications was probably experienced as more exciting at that time than it would be now.

In order to avoid legal difficulties, the COC at first did not permit persons under 21 years of age to join. The membership in these years was, moreover, predominantly male.

9. Anonymous (1949), Beschermt de jeugd! (Protect the youth!) *Vriendschap* (Friendship), *4*, (4), 13.

10. Brunoz was the pseudonym of Edward Brongersma, who from 1972 onward also published on pedophilia under his own name. He has made, and continues to make, important contributions to the emancipation of pedophilia.

11. See note 5.

12. The International Committee for Sexual Equality was founded in the Netherlands in order to bring about international cooperation between homophile organizations. Due to the lack of strength of the other participating organizations, the Committee ceased existence within a few years.

13. See Salden, M., op. cit.

14. The "expert" was the criminologist Professor Pompe, writing in a special issue of the magazine devoted to Article 248-bis. The issue was entitled, strangely enough, indecent assault against minors. The other contributions opposed the seduction theory and called for the repeal of the Article.

15. This report was prepared by the National Health Council, an official advisory council to the Netherlands government concerning issues of mental and physical public health.

16. Anonymous, 1971, Advies Gezondheidsraad inzake 248bis. (Advice of the Health Council related to 248bis.) *Informatie Bulletin Dialoog* (Information Bulletin Dialogue), *4*, (3), 82-84.

17. Schofield, M. (1965). *Social aspects of homosexuality*. London: Longman. In this study, in which pedophiles were referred to as "child molesters," Schofield compared, among other things, men who were imprisoned for homosexual contacts with other adults (21 years and older) with men imprisoned for sexual contacts with boys under 16. Besides the fact that he found no significant differences in their backgrounds, his findings could, moreover, in no way be generalized to all homosexuals and all pedophiles, because of his overly selective sample.

18. Tielman, R. (1982). *Homoseksualiteit in Nederland* (Homosexuality in The Netherlands). Meppel: Boom.

19. Onstenk, A. (1983). Van brede schouders tot hoge hakken: Veranderende

beeldvorming over lesbische vrouwen in de periode 1939-1965. (From broad shoulders to high heels: Changing images of lesbian women in the period 1939-1965.) Amsterdam: SUA (Student Press Amsterdam).

20. Like the COC, the NVSH was founded in 1946 as the post-war continuation of the Nieuw Malthusiaanse Bond (New Malthusian League), which had been active predominantly in promoting birth-control education. The principal aim of the present-day NVSH is "the emancipation of individuals and community in a sexual perspective." Initially, the NVSH was rather heterosexually oriented.

21. Just as gays came out of the closets, pedophiles come out of the bushes in raincoats with candy. An important event in this connection was the public congress *Pedophilia and Society,* organized by pedophiles in 1977 in cooperation with the Dutch National Center for Public Mental Health.

22. Tielman, R. (1977), Niemand is heilig. (Nobody is saintly.) *COC-Sek, 7,* (6), 9-10.

23. The COC congress is the highest policy-making body in that organization. It convenes yearly to evaluate the plans and the functioning of the executive committee.

Gay SM in Pornography and Reality

A. X. van Naerssen
Mart van Dijk
Geert Hoogeveen
Dick Visser
Gertjan van Zessen
University of Utrecht

ABSTRACT. A picture of SM interactions as depicted by pornographical issues of SM between 1974 and 1983 is presented by means of a correlational study of pornography. Actual SM scenarios are then compared with the depiction in magazines. The changes that have occurred over more than a decade reflected changes in the nature of violence and sexuality.

Toward the end of the 1960s, the number of Dutch pornographic magazines quickly increased. Over a short period approximately 100 monthlies were published, most of which did not survive a year. At the same time, the first Dutch homo-pornographic magazines appeared. Besides photographs and contact ads, they featured stories. We investigated four well-known Dutch gay magazines (*Boy Smile, David Boy, Jack*, and *Binky*) that came out between January 1970 and April 1983. During this period these magazines published 398 stories that could be labeled pornographic, i.e., sexual contacts between males were described in detail. A number of cases concerned interactions in which the male roles were unequal, one being dominant and the

Mart van Dijk, Geert Hoogeveen, Dick Visser, and Gertjan van Zessen studied Psychology at the University of Utrecht. The present study was part of a research program they helped conduct on sado-masochism. Correspondence may be addressed to the authors, Vakgroep Klinische Psychologie, Postbus 80140, 3508 TC, University of Utrecht, The Netherlands.

111

other submissive. Those stories, a total of 136, we called SM-pornography. The correlation between the SM stories and the time, 1970-1983, was .93, which led us to conclude that the amount of SM in homo-pornographic magazines appearing in that time period increased significantly.

THE SM-SCENARIO

The theme most frequently recurring in the 136 SM-pornographic stories was mental humiliation, in which the dominating partner abuses the submissive partner, or disparages him, or gives degrading orders (such as eating from a dog-pan). Mental humiliation occurred 428 times; it was absent in only 24 stories. Fornicating the submissive partner was described 176 times in 107 stories. Other highly frequent acts were bondage (133 times), flagellation (126 times), fellatio by the submissive partner (119 times), licking the leader's body (109 times), and caressing the submissive partner (119 times). An SM-scenario was divided into acts that stressed the vulnerability and humiliation of the submissive partner, although in a number of stories sexual interactions also took place in an atmosphere of caressing and tenderness. A limited number of stories we investigated boiled down to an enumeration of purely violent, sexual interactions, most of which were a combination of humiliating and more romantic acts. During the period 1970-1983, the frequency of the acts mentioned above did not increase, nor were the correlations of SM acts within the period significant. What we did see, however, was that in this particular period a number of "new" acts were described (fisting, bestiality, the use of amyl nitrate), whereas sex with urine (water sports, golden shower), which was described earlier, suddenly occurred much more frequently. The total frequency of these acts was low (fisting—6, bestiality—11, amyl nitrate—11, urolagnia—39), but they played an important role in the stories in which they were described.

Other Characteristics

The SM story usually was told by the submissive partner (84), followed by the dominating partner (32), or a third person (20), which might have indicated that the authors expected their readers to identify with the submissive role. The partners usually did not know each other at the beginning of the story, but by its conclusion they generally parted friends. In only six cases did the submissive partner make clear he was not interested in having further contact with his partner. Also, there was a definite physical difference between the men involved in an SM interaction. The disparity between the dominating and submissive roles was not expressed in terms of masculine and feminine, but instead ranged from very masculine to boyish.

Voluntariness

Masters and Johnson's (1979) research revealed that some spontaneous sexual fantasies of both heterosexuals and homosexuals, male and female, are focused on enforced sexual interactions. On the whole, those fantasizing identify with the one on whom the sexual contact is imposed. For the homosexual men (80) within this study, these fantasies often included bondage and flagellation. These data, however, did not provide us with insight into the degree of voluntariness the "victim" displayed in the interaction. We attempted to analyze this aspect of the fantasy in the SM stories; to this end we divided each story into three parts.

1. *The introduction.* How was the contact between the dominating and submissive partner established? Was, for example, the submissive partner unable to resist, and thus involuntarily submitted to the dominating partner, or did he take part in the SM-interaction of his own accord? This aspect was scored as voluntary or compulsory, per story.

2. *The sexual interactions.* How did the submissive partner experience the interaction? Did he wish to escape it, or did he submit to, and even enjoy, his humiliations, bondage, and flagellation? This aspect was also scored as voluntary or compulsory, per story.

3. *The evaluation of the SM interaction.* Here we paid attention to submissive partner's attitude *after* the interaction. Did he value the situation as positive or negative? (See Tables 1 and 2.)

In the period 1970-1974, the number of stories in which talk of compulsion occurred turned out to be relatively high (50%),

---

Table 1*

Evaluation of SM Interactions

Introduction	Sexual Interaction	Evaluation	Total Score
Compulsory	Compulsory	Negative	1
Compulsory	Voluntary	Negative	2
Voluntary	Compulsory	Negative	
Voluntary	Voluntary	Negative	3
Compulsory	Compulsory	Positive	4
Compulsory	Compulsory	Positive	5
Voluntary	Compulsory	Positive	
Voluntary	Voluntary	Positive	6

---

*Table 1 reflects this score system. The results of the evaluation of the SM interaction weighed heavily in assessing the total score.

Table 2*

Degree of the Submissive Partner's Voluntariness in the SM

Interaction

		N	%
1.	Mercilessly compulsory	20	14.7
2.	Compulsory	3	2.2
3.	Rather compulsory	1	0.7
4.	Rather voluntary	20	14.7
5.	Voluntary	35	25.7
6.	Very Voluntary	57	41.9

*Table 2 reflects the results of this score system applied to the

136 SM stories.

whereas in the following period (1975-1983) this dropped to 20%. In other words, in 80% of the stories the submissive partner was said to value the SM-interaction as predominantly positive afterwards.

Hardness

At the outset of our research, we expected that not only had the frequency of SM stories in pornographic literature increased, but also their hardness, violence, and brutality. These aspects were taken into consideration when each story was scored on a hardness scale ranging from 1 (soft) to 6 (very hard). A story was considered very hard if it described severe mutilations, rapes, injuries, as well as complete coercion of the submissive partner. Eighteen percent of the stories fell into the hard to very hard category. This category peaked during the period 1970-1974. The correlation between time and hardness was −.16 (p = .04), thus the relative hardness of the stories decreased after 1974.

Summary

Sadism, as described in the classic "120 Days of Sodom" by Marquis de Sade, implies that victims are entirely delivered up to the power of the leader, who expresses his power sexually by humiliating and torturing his inferior. The scenario of this type of sadistic pornography emphasizes the victim's complete defenselessness. The fear, disgust, and pain of the victim stimulate the sexual lusts of the victimizer. The gay SM scenarios in the pornographic stories we investigated up to 1974 met these criteria in about 50% of the cases. In stories appearing after 1974, the emotional context of the stories changed: The interaction was desired by both parties, the acts grew less hard, and the SM scenario showed SM acts combined with affectionate and caressing ones. In addition, diversity of the situations described was altogether wider. In the most recent stories we investigated, there were very hard stories indeed, in which the participation of the submissive partner was described as voluntary, but there were also rather softer stories which included talk of compulsion.

GAY SM IN REALITY

According to Visser's inquiry in 1983, 45 of the 400 sado-masochistically inclined men that were investigated considered themselves exclusively or predominantly homosexual. Of this homosexual group, 14 regarded themselves as predominantly or exclusively masochistic, 23 as predominantly sadistic, and 8 as equally sadistic and masochistic. In the interviews we had with 16 of the 45 homosexuals, the subjects we discussed primarily concerned the SM experience: the ways contacts were made, the structure of the sexual interactions, and their evaluation. The average age of the men interviewed was 40.9 years. Of this subgroup, 10 preferred the role of the submissive, and 6 that of the dominating partner. Yet with all 16 there was talk of a relative preference, i.e., the role they played was dependent on the situation, their moods, or the partner's wishes. Only three men had exclusively sado-masochistic interactions with a regular partner. The others had several partners they met through contact-ads, leather SM bars, gay social nights, or SM clubs. The majority of the respondents indicated that mental humiliation in the interaction did not suffice in itself; some type of physical humiliation, especially bondage and flagellation, was also essential. All but one of the 16 men reported alternating between hardness and tenderness but, contrary to the descriptions in pornographic literature, the tenderness was provided by the submissive partner. Another striking difference between situations from pornographic literature and reports from those interviewed was that for those interviewed, having an orgasm, either through fornication, fellatio, or masturbation, was not essential during an SM encounter. Instead, the satisfaction was derived from non-orgastic aspects of the interaction. The terms agreed on before starting an interaction varied according to the phase the contact was in. Once an agreement was reached on having an SM interaction, and on the roles, the type of acts and their intensity were then decided upon.

Only two respondents were avowed fetishists, one with a preference for wrestling, the other with a preference for rubber boots, preferences which for these two men were essential to any of their SM interactions. The other 14 limited themselves to global agreements in which mental humiliation, bondage, and flagellation were ever-recurring elements, without specifying in advance the ways these elements would be realized in the interaction. Improvisation and playfulness were highly appreciated. Also, the one taking the submissive role upon himself should be allowed to stop the interaction if he wished so because, for these men, fixing the boundaries within which this game of power and powerlessness took place was the quintessence of SM interaction. In practice, neither the dominating nor the submissive partner would know beforehand what degree of humiliation or pain would be bearable, so the limits were, in essence, determined during the game. Such an understanding presupposed a basic trust between the participants in a SM interaction.

Of the few hundred interactions reported to us in interviews, only two were called too hard, which meant that the dominating partner had continued in spite of his partner asking to end the SM interaction. Adult men were preferred as partners. Those younger than 31 were considered less interesting because they were said often to interrupt the progress of an interaction on account of their lack of experience, incertitudes, fears, or inadequacy in reacting to signals. This differs from SM pornographic literature, in which a relatively large number of submissive partners are described as being boyish.

CONCLUSION

Pornography is based primarily on sexual fantasy. Thus, in view of his commercial interests, the producer of pornography is compelled to be aware of, and attempt to complement, the fantasies of prospective buyers. In this sense, pornographic literature reflects the social values and standards of the society in which it is produced. The changes in SM pornographic literature between 1970 and 1983 may be seen as changes taking place in the ideas and fantasies about violence and sexuality between men. Within the period we investigated, strictly sadistic interactions as described by de Sade, which focus on the sexual excitement of the dominating partner, appeared to have changed into sadomasochistic interactions, forms of sexual relations that allowed all parties involved to fix the scenario. In practice the SM scenarios proved to bear much resemblance to the scenarios described in SM pornographic literature, with the exception that, at least according to those SM participants we interviewed, in practice there was always talk of domination, submissiveness, violence, and inequality being *acted*. Irrespective of their roles, persons taking part in SM interactions must subject themselves to a social code which does justice to the expectations and desires of all partners involved. This is definitely different from pornographic fiction, in which it is the reader who eventually decides whether a code is sexually interesting.

REFERENCES

Masters, W. H., & Johnson, V. E. (1979). *Homosexuality in perspective.* Boston: Little, Brown.
Visser, D. (1983). *Vormen van Sadomasochisme; deel 1: Onderzoeksresultaten.* Utrecht: University of Utrecht.

Reading About Homosexuality

Page F. Grubb

ABSTRACT. A study was conducted to access the importance of reading about experiences on homosexuality for adolescents and post-adolescents. Although no conclusive evidence could be found to link their reading experience to later experiences as a means of instigating change or providing role models, the author suggests that reading materials can be influential.

Reading is often cited in the literature on homosexuality as an important source of information on homosexuality.[1] The following is a report of some of the findings of a research project undertaken to assess the actual importance of reading for adolescent and post-adolescent experiences of homosexuality, and an attempt to sketch the social inbedding of reading for a group of gay readers.

The project was designed as an exploratory-descriptive research on the role of reading in perception-forming processes, focusing on perception-forming with regard to homosexuality. Such processes were conceived of as ongoing in nature, i.e., not finalized at the first point of self-definition and manifestation.[2] A questionnaire was developed to obtain information on respondents' experiences of homosexuality, and to understand the process leading up to self-definition as homosexual, general patterns in cultural recreation (including reading), and gay-related patterns in cultural recreation (including reading).

Respondents were recruited from members of and visitors to the Dutch Society for the Integration of Homosexuality, the

Page F. Grubb is currently writing on a full-time basis. Correspondence may be addressed to the author, c/o The Deanery, 1103 Main Street, Davenport, IA 52803.

COC, to obtain respondents who were actively homosexual. In addition, respondents were recruited with the stated requirement that they be interested in filling out a lengthy questionnaire on reading habits. Both men and women filled in the questionnaire. Respondents tended to be "active" and "cadre" members of the COC, devoting five or more hours per week to movement activities, and were open about their homosexuality. An excess of 65% of the respondents' family members knew about their homosexuality, as well as 65% of their colleagues and 58% of their neighbors. Applying the terminology of Moerings and Straver (1970), respondents were characterized as being largely middle to high manifestors.

Despite the fact that respondents tended to follow political developments related to homosexuality more closely than cultural matters, they stated that they were fairly well aware of the opportunities for reading books and viewing films featuring homosexuality. They kept informed about such possibilities via homosexual friends, and via both the gay and non-gay press. They reported reading an average of 17 books per year for recreation, out of which 3.5 books tended to feature homosexuality, and 9.5 books per year for information, out of which one concerned homosexuality. At least 25% of the respondents came from a milieu in which reading as a recreational activity could not be assumed to be endemic.

Two sets of exercises were performed with data obtained. In the first exercise, material obtained on respondents' experiences with homosexuality was correlated with various studies on homosexual self-exploratory processes by Dank (1971), Lee (1977), Harry and DeVall (1978), Cass (1979), Coleman (1982), De Koning (1967), Sanders (1968, 1977), Moerings and Straver (1970), van der Feen and Sanders (1980), Bohlander and Monnich (1980), and others. The attempt here was to research some of the ways in which respondents experienced daily matters related to homosexuality, so as to be able to contrast these with their encounters with homosexuality while reading.

The second exercise consisted of correlating data obtained on reading experiences with various studies on the esthetics and the semiotics of reading processes by Iser (1972/1974), Jauss (1970, 1977), Warning (1975), Koeller (1977), Klinger (1978), Holland (1978), and others. In such stories the literary transaction has been profitably researched from the viewpoint of perception-forming and the experience of "the intensity of meaningfulness" (Koeller, 1977). Through correlating our findings with the above-mentioned studies, we hoped to be able to conduct field research within various theoretical frameworks, including reception studies (the study of the way texts are experienced by readers in differing social and historical constellations), semiotics, the sociology of literature, and the psychology of reading. We attempted to interpret the impact a number of book titles had had on respondents, with these books being viewed both as esthetic objects and as potential sources of "information" on homosexuality, and of experiences involving varying degrees of the "intensity of meaningfulness."

The first exercise resulted in a number of negative findings which were interesting in and of themselves. Further, they were crucial for the way this project could proceed. Our findings may be summarized by grouping them under two headings: (a) the importance of reading for the experience of homosexuality; and, (b) the experience of reading about homosexuality.[3]

THE IMPORTANCE OF READING FOR THE EXPERIENCE OF HOMOSEXUALITY

Almost half, 47%, of the respondents reported that reading furnished their primary source of information on homosexuality during adolescence, a period in which their peer group was not homosexual. However, the more they became involved in a homosexual "interaction network" (Tielman, 1982), the less reading was cited as a source of information on homosexuality. These sources became gay liberation journals (40%), homosexual friends (33.3%), and newspapers and periodicals (20%). We asked ourselves whether the degree of importance given to reading during adolescence as a source of information on homosexuality might not reflect two rather different things: either a paucity of other sources of information during adolescence, or the status reading held as a valued activity they wanted to engage in to a significant degree.[4] We came to the following conclusions. We were not willing to see reading as a unique, socially isolated source of information on homosexuality during adolescence, even for the 47% group, and in general we came to concur with Moerings and Straver's (1970) finding that literature as a source of information is subordinate in importance to interpersonal communication, even for the 47% group, for several reasons.

We found, for example, that respondents quite actively used libraries and peer group leads to obtain the material which provided them with information on homosexuality. However, we found that such material could not be thought of as "gay" literature. The median age at which our respondents began sharing their insights into themselves as homosexual with others was 20.8. We obtained the titles of only three books which had been read before this age; in reading these titles, direct statements on homosexuality were not registered at all (Blaman, 1948/1960; Salinger, 1951/1978), and same-sex relationships were not characterized as involving homosexuality (Haasse, 1948/1974).

In general, respondents, and specifically the younger respondents, had not consciously recognized direct statements on homosexuality when they read a book. (See also, Baldwin, 1956/1974.) Highly stylized presentations of homosexuality (Couperus, 1905/1974; Mann, 1912/1965; Wilde, 1891/1981) were sometimes not recognized as presentations of homosexuality; neither were presentations of homosexuality as an anomalous situation ('t Hart, 1973/1978; Membrecht, 1969; Reve, 1969, 1972, 1973), particularly where the "anomaly" of homosexuality could be reduced to a purely sexual act, or a blurring of distinctions between various, non-heterosexual, forms of sexuality.

Again, the presence of same-sex friendships or relationships in a text did not automatically lead to either absorption in a text or to the conclusion that homosexuality was being featured. (See also, Mann, 1912/1965; Wilde, 1891/1981.) Neither was the known homosexuality of an author sufficient for a reader to perceive homosexuality in a text (Wilde, 1891/1981; Burnier, 1969; Blaman, 1948/1960). The attempt to "metaphorize" homosexuality in a text (Burnier, 1969) did not always enable the reader to transcend what might be problematical in that text's presentation of homosexuality, and to proceed from the specific to the general in sexuality.

We interpreted such findings as meaning that, particularly during adolescence, reading was fairly random. The "information" obtained from books would have been of an eclectic, nonspecific, and abstract sort, and would require the catalyst of social testing to solidify it to the point where the individual could perceive that information as information at all, and specifically as information on homosexuality. In fact, homosexuality probably would not have been consciously perceived in books. Instead, reading was engaged in as a "supplementary and channelizing activity" (Straver, 1977), and to consolidate a general feeling of "being different" from others, a feeling which had first come to respondents at a median age of 11.9 years, and had developed through social interaction; specifically, the awareness that they had interests or behaved in ways which were contrary to what they felt was expected of them.[5]

Just as respondents did not become aware of being different from others through reading, but used reading in an attempt to focus on what that difference meant, they did not decide that their "difference" was their homosexuality based on their reading experience. In fact, they only consciously set out to read specifically about homosexuality once they had decided that their difference was indeed their homosexuality.

Yet even after they defined themselves as homosexual, our respondents' lives were hardly monopolized by their sexuality.

We attempted to discern if anything could be said about the way homosexuality figured in respondents' general recreational preferences, and queried them on their use of subcultural facilities (i.e., bars, saunas, women's and men's houses, cruising areas, social visiting with homosexual friends) as compared to general cultural facilities (i.e., theatre, movies, museums, concerts, family and social visiting with heterosexual relations and acquaintances). In addition, we attempted to see whether respondents' adolescent experiences of homosexuality[6] correlated in any way with patterns in cultural recreation. Other factors we tried to correlate were age, religious affiliation and amount of participation in church-related activities, manifestation ("who knows you're gay"), general awareness of gay political events and gay cultural events, amount of gay versus general reading activity and cinema attendance, and the use of pornography.

Our findings were largely negative. We found no meaningful patterns in cultural recreation, and no fixed way in which respondents proportioned their time between gay and non-gay activities.[7] There was no correlation between the adolescent experiences of sexuality and any of the above variables, including preferences for specific books or the experience of specific books and films. One correlation we did find was that the more respondents read, the more they tended to go to the movies, and the more they tended to be aware of where homosexuality was to be found in society. But while it was true that one of five books read for recreational purposes did feature homosexuality, we found no percentual increase which would suggest that the more books respondents read, the more books they read which featured homosexuality. We did find that the more responsibility respondents were given in their gay movement activities, the more time they tended to invest in them. But while homosexuality might have provided a basis for the organization of their political (gay movement) activities, it by no means "organized" respondents' recreational activities nor their reading.

The above negative findings had three consequences for our

project. First, we were able to dispense with looking for a kind of "sensibility," such as might have emerged had we found common patterns among our respondents' use of recreational facilities, their adolescent and current experiences of homosexuality, preferences for certain "types" of books, and so forth. Second, we were able to qualify the theory (Klinger, 1978) that it is simply a "current concern," such as realizing one's homosexuality in social behavior, which a text signals and speaks to in a reading and which causes that text to "come alive" for a reader. In fact, we concluded that for any given reading experience, an author's intention to write about homosexuality need not necessarily be perceived by a reader, no matter how explicit that intention might be. And we concluded that a reader's intention to become informed about homosexuality would not always be met during the reading act, nor need it be, for one's personal homosexuality would not always be the motivating force behind a reader's cultural pursuits. Third, we were forced to concentrate on the intensity with which texts were experienced as meaningful, and to interpret a number of texts from the point of view of the degree of meaningfulness they afforded, as opposed to a point of view which would tend to assume a direct correlation between the way homosexuality figures in readers' lives and the way it figured in their reading experiences.[8]

EXPERIENCES OF READING
ABOUT HOMOSEXUALITY

In general, we would state that respondents' literary experiences with homosexuality were much less distinct than their day-to-day ones, in the sense that respondents were generally less sure that homosexuality was involved in what they read than they were that homosexuality was involved in the activities of their daily lives; this is not so much due to respondents being careless readers as to the fact that not every book featuring homosexuality which they read featured homosexuality in a way which was relevant to them, and in a way which helped them develop their personal perception and experience of homosexuality.

We found that books which respondents experienced with the greatest intensity of meaningfulness and which offered readers a conscious experience of homosexuality (A. J. A. H., 1971; Harten, 1974, 1886; 't Hart, 1973/1978) were books which offered possibilities for dynamic identification,[9] and which were complex in that they depicted sexuality from different angles and as operating in various spheres. Such books evoked resistance by directing the readers' attention to opinions about homosexuality which must have been at odds with respondents' experiences of it. Examples of this would include: Sex is the most important thing in realizing a gay lifestyle (A. J. A. H., 1971); Homosexuality is a distant, obscure, and vaguely troubling phenomenon (Harten, 1964/1970); Extremes of behavior, such as transvestism and sadism, characterize homosexuality (Harten, 1968/1969; 't Hart, 1973/1978); Unless one has money, youthful good looks are everything (Harten, 1968/1969); Homosexuals cannot be "real" men and women ('t Hart, 1973/1978). In these three texts, attention was called to such matters, which then evoked resistance in the readers. Readers were then, as it were, required to make their own emotive link between the behavior of protagonists and their own imagined ability to engage in behavior corresponding to their sense of themselves. Through an act of the imagination, which is usually referred to as identification, respondents were able to direct their attention to matters which were potentially threatening, and to have those threats defused. Respondents could overcome the resistance evoked by these three texts, but only after they dealt with the matters evoking resistance. In this way readers could consciously use these texts in their perception-forming processes on homosexuality.

There were, however, several instances in which books experienced with an intense degree of meaningfulness could not be interpreted as having contributed directly to perception-forming on homosexuality. In their experience with these particular titles (Baldwin, 1956/1977; Couperus, 1905/1974; Mann, 1912/1965; Salinger, 1951/1978; Wilde, 1891/1981), respondents apparently were not able to see the behavior depicted as homosexually related; thus, although these books were experienced as complex, that complexity was not perceived as including homosexuality. Similarly, the identification which took place was not homosexually related; the resistance these texts evoked had little to do with cognitive material on homosexuality. Here, the imaginative act of identification might have focused on a situation or a mood, rather than behavior. This might have been the reason why homosexuality did not surface in respondents' experience of a text.

We found a number of texts which had been experienced with only a medium intensity of meaningfulness. Once again, these texts could be divided into two groups. In the first group (Burnier, 1969; Reve, 1969; van Manen, 1979), homosexuality was consciously perceived, but these texts were not experienced as complex with regard to homosexuality. The form of identification which occurred was trivial: The books seemed to be confirming what respondents already knew, and little resistance was evoked. In the second group of texts (Blaman, 1948/1960, 1960/1961), homosexuality was not consciously perceived. These books were probably too complex, but that complexity was not perceived as involving homosexuality; thus, identification and resistance were minimal.

Finally, we found a group of texts which had been experienced with a low intensity of meaningfulness. In two texts (Reve, 1972, 1973), homosexuality was perceived in concrete terms. Although these texts evoked a great deal of resistance in the readers, the texts were not experienced as complex, and thus little or no identification took place. We might hypothesize that these books did not allow the resolution of the resistance they evoked, or perhaps the resistance our respondents felt was directed at finding these books' presentation of homosexuality relevant to their own experience of the ''meaning'' of homosexuality. They could see homosexuality here, but wanted to have little to do with it.

Two other texts (Haasse, 1948/1974; Membrecht, 1969) were not experienced as involving homosexuality. There was no identification with them, and no sense of complexity perceived in the case of the Membrecht text. Whatever resistance there was to both texts was not evoked by the texts' presentation of homosexuality, as such a presentation was not perceived. Indeed, Membrecht's text occasioned a great deal of irritation, as if respondents sensed that the author wanted to talk about homosexuality but did so only indirectly.

CONCLUSION

We cannot conclude that respondents' reading habits grew less critical the older they grew, nor can we say anything about books functioning as role-models or about books instigating change in readers. Yet we submit that these matters are related. If we associate a positive reading experience with trivial forms of identification, then, as we have seen, such forms of identification do not result in high intensities of meaningfulness. When these identifications do occur, the factor of resistance tends to ensure that a text's homosexual subject matter will be read critically. Further, we have seen that a process of perception-forming can be honed, as it were, through reading, but never initiated and never rounded-off. Without social testing, whatever perception-forming reading may help foster will remain inconclusive, non-viable in terms of social reality. Indeed, we may hypothesize that any literary encounter with, or experience of homosexuality will remain inconclusive in all but esthetic terms until that experience is corroborated by social experience.

And finally, we cannot draw any firm conclusions about the

concept of sensibility, something which would help researchers understand the ways homosexuals lead their lives and how their thinking patterns influence, and are influenced by, their sexuality. We simply found no evidence of such a mechanism,[10] either in the recreational activities respondents pursued and the books they read, or in the ways we construed their experience of these books.

If there is such a thing as a gay sensibility, we submit that it is to be found in a person's readiness to find certain sign-material relevant to the perception-forming processes related to homosexuality. But this sign-material is not one monolithic chunk of cultural matter, and perception-forming processes are not identical with regard to either cultural input or perceptual output. It is true that the amount and type of cultural material society makes available for perception-forming purposes does tend to be controlled by various sociological and political mechanisms. And we may assume that sensibilities may be organized through such mechanisms (by means of the individual testing his sensibilities against social realities) to result in certain organized forms of personal taste, such as trends, fashions, and an insistence on certain forms of style. But these are ideological matters which say nothing about a psychic base for response or for activities related to perception-forming. It was precisely this psychic base about which we could not reach any tangible conclusions.

NOTES

1. See Straver (1977, pp. 32, 148); Sengers (1969, p. 196); Sanders (1977, pp. 84-85); van der Feen & Sanders (1980, p. 25); Harry & DeVall (1978, p. 65); Dank (1971, pp. 184, 188-189); Cass (1979, pp. 222-223); Moerings & Straver (1970, p. 71ff); Bohlander & Monnich (1980, pp. 41, 66, 123); Bauer (1980, p. 5); Bergh, Bjerk, Lund (1978, pp. 21-22); Spada (1979, pp. 24, 27, 28); Jay & Young (1977, pp. 55, 108, 110, 112).
2. In a more extensive study from which this article has been excerpted (Grubb, 1983), this approach to homosexuality as an ongoing matter for perception-forming

was termed an "open-ended" approach. It was largely derived from a study of Dutch theorists, and contrasted with a more "linear-progressive" model used by many North American theorists.

3. There are numerous ideological matters involved in gay reading which cannot be dealt with in this paper. See also Grubb (1983) for a detailed interpretation of the way 16 books by Dutch, American, English, and German authors were read.

4. Respondents also consistently reported having read more during adolescence for the categories of novels, study books, and general periodicals and newspapers than did either their parents or siblings.

5. Of the respondents, 40% gave this response to the query "how did you notice you were different from others"; 26% mentioned feelings of attraction to members of the same sex; 12% mentioned homosexuality as such.

6. We were able to obtain median ages for various events in the adolescent experience of homosexuality. The first awareness of being different from others occurred at 11.9 years; first discovery of something like homosexuality in oneself at 14.9 years; first gathering of information on homosexuality at 17.6 years (we interpreted this information as actually diffuse in nature); first contact (not necessarily sexual) with other gay people at 18.7 years; first gay sexual experience at 19.2 years; first active pursuit of sexual contacts at 20.3 years; and first acknowledgement of own homosexuality to others at 20.8. In addition, we were able to "type" the adolescent experiences of homosexuality by correlating the amount of time the respondent had taken to experience all the above events with the age at which the respondent began the experience of homosexuality. We found that most respondents could be divided between two types of experience; one got off to a late start and took a short period of time to experience the above events; the other group began at an early age and took a long time to experience all the above events. (An early start was from 0-11 years of age, a late start from 12-30; a short period of time to experience the above events was 1-10 years; a longer period of time 11-30.) However, there was no correlation between type of adolescent experience of homosexuality and any other factor studied. In general, we had to conclude that the above "typology" was fairly meaningless, certainly in terms of any effect the adolescent experience of homosexuality would be presumed to have had on further development, including tastes in cultural matters and the way lifestyles evolve to accommodate sexual preference.

7. The only two correlations found were somewhat trivial: Those who tended to frequent the theater tended to frequent concert halls in the same degree; the same held for devotees of outdoor cruising and indoor sex in back rooms.

8. The intensity of meaningfulness was interpreted by comparing scores given for a book in general, and for its presentation of homosexuality specifically. Book and film titles were also subjected to cluster analyses, and title-clusters further facilitated our interpretive work. See Grubb (1983).

9. Following Straver (1977), identification is an imaginative act centering on behavior, behavior which one can imagine oneself engaging in whether one had ever engaged (or would ever engage) in that behavior. Following Koller (1977), "trivial" forms of identification exclude innovation in perception-forming, while "dynamic" forms of identification involve a subject "already caught up in an attempt to create certain structural orderings (perceptions, PFG) without yet having broken the resistance accompanying such attempts." It is to Koeller that we are indebted for the concept that resistance, identification, and complexity are the ingredients necessary for the intense experience of meaningfulness.

10. Compare the relatively early finding by Evelyn Hooker (1957) that homosexuality as a psychological entity simply does not exist.

REFERENCES

Primary Sources

Amsterdamse Jongeren Aktie-groepen Homoseksualiteit (1971). *Jongen-jongen/ meisfe-meisje.* 's-Gravenhage: Stichting Uitgerij NVSH.

Baldwin, J. (1977). *Giovannie's Room.* London: Corgi Books. (Original work published 1965)

Blaman, A. (1960). *Eenzaam avontuur.* Amsterdam: J. M. Meulenhoff. (Original work published 1948)

Blaman, A. (1961). *De Verliezers.* Amsterdam: J. M. Meulenhoff. (Original work published 1960)

Burnier, A. (1969). *Het jongensuur.* Amsterdam: Em. Querido.

Couperus, L. (1974). *De Berg van Licht.* Wageningen: L. J. Veen. (Original work published 1905)

Haasse, H. (1974). *Oeroeg.* Amsterdam: Em. Querido. (Original work published 1948)

't Hart, M. (1978). *Ik had een wapenbroeder.* Amsterdam: De Arbeiderspers. (Original work published 1973)

Harten, J. (1970). *Operatie Montycoat.* In *Operatie Montycoat, Verhalen.* Amsterdam: De Bezige Bij. (Original work published 1964)

Harten, J. (1969). *De getatoeeerde Lorelei.* Amsterdam: De Bezige Bij. (Original work published 1968)

Manen, J. van (1979). *Verliefd.* Amsterdam: Em. Querido.

Mann, T. (1965). Der Tod in Venedig. In *Der Tod in Venedig und andere Erzaellungen.* Frankfurt am Main: Fischer Buecherei. (Original work published 1912)

Membrecht, S. (1969). *27 verhalen uit de homosuele sfeer.* Amsterdam: Uitgeverij Contact.

Reve, G. (1969). *Nader tot U.* Amsterdam: G. A. van Oorschot.

Reve, G. (1972). *De Taal der liefde.* Amsterdam: Polak & Van Gennep.

Reve, G. (1973). *Lieve jongens.* Amsterdam: Polak & Van Gennep.

Salinger, J. D. (1978). *The catcher in the rye.* Harmondsworth, Penguin Books. (Original work published 1951)

Wilde, O. (1981). *The picture of Dorian Gray.* Oxford: Oxford University Press. (Original work published 1891)

Secondary Sources

Bauer, K. S. (1980). *Sozialisationsbedingungen in Homosexuellengruppen.* Entwurf fur ein Forschungsdesign. Dortmund: Manuskript.

Bergh, S., Bjerck, B., & Lund, E. (1978). *Homofile. Myter og Verkelighet. En undersoksel blant homofile kvinner og menn i Norge.* Oslo: Pax Forlag.

Bohlaender, C., & Moennich, H. (1980). *Zur psychischen Verarbeitung des coming out bei mannlichen Homosexuellen. Die Bedeutung von Entwicklungskonflikten fur das Selbstbild.* Berlin: Diplomarbeit beim Pscychologischen Institut.

Cass, V. C. (1979). Homosexuality identity formation: A theoretical model. *Journal of Homosexuality, 4,* 219-236.

Coleman, E. (1982). Developmental stages of the coming out process. *Journal of Homosexuality, 7*(2/3), 31-43.

Dank, B. M. (1971). Coming out in the gay world. *Psychiatry, 34,* 180-197.

Feen, R.-J. van der, & Sanders, G. (1980). *Homoseksuele jongeren en hun ouders.* Deventer: Van Logham Slaterus.

Grubb, P. F. (1983). *You got it from all those books. A study of gay reading.* Unpublished doctoral dissertation, University of Amsterdam.

Harry, J., & DeVall, W. B. (1978). *The social organization of gay males.* New York: Prager.

Holland, N. N. (1978). A transactive account of transactive criticism. *Poetics, 1,* 177-189.

Hooker, E. (1957). The adjustments of the male overt homosexual. *Journal of Projective Techniques, 21,* 18-31.

Iser, W. (1974). *The implied reader. Patterns of communication in prose fiction from Bunyan to Beckett.* Baltimore: Johns Hopkins University Press. (Original work published 1972)

Jauss, H. R. (1970). *Literaturgeschichte als Provokation.* Frankfurt am Main: Suhrkamp Verlag.

Jauss, H. R. (1977). *Asthetische Erfahrung und literarische Hermeneutik I.* Munchen: Verlag.

Jay, K., & Young, A. (1977). *The gay report: Lesbians and gay men speak out about sexual experiences and lifestyles.* New York: Summit Books.

Klinger, E. (1978). The flow of thought and its implications for literary communication. *Poetics, 7,* 191-205.

Koeller, W. (1977). Der sprachteoretische Wert des semiotischen Zeichenmodellls. In K. H. Spinner (Ed.), *Zeichen, text, sinn. Zur Semiotik des literarischen Verstehens* (pp. 7-77). Gottingen: Vandenhoeck & Ruprecht.

Koning, P. P. J. de (1967). *Een kwalitatieve analyse van de levensgeschiedenis van een aantal homosexuelen.* Groningen: Instituut voor Sociale Psychologie.

Lee. J. A. (1977). A study in the sociology of homosexual liberation. *Journal of Homosexuality, 3,* 49-78.

Moerings, M., & Straver, C. J. (1970). *Homofiele jongeren in relatie tot hun omgeving.* Zeist: N. E. S. S. O.

Sanders, G. J. E. M. (1968). De zelfbeleving als uitdagingssituatie. *Een kwalitatieve analyse van de levensloop van een aantal personen die zichzelf als homofiel beschouwen.* Groningen: Instituut voor Sociale Psychologie.

Sanders, G. J. E. M. (1977). *Het gewone en het bijzondere van de homoseksuele leefsituatie.* Deventer: Van Loghum Slaterus.

Sengers, W. J. (1969). *Homosexualiteit als klacht.* Bussum: Paul Brand.

Spada, J. (1979). *The Spada report. The newest survey of gay male sexuality.* New York: Signet Books.

Straver, C. J. (1967). *Massacommunicatie en godsdienstige beinvloeding.* Unpublished doctoral dissertation, University of Groningen.

Straver, C. J. (1977). Sex-uitbeelding en sex-verbeelding. Zeist: N.I.S.S.O.

Tielman, R. (1982). *Homoseksualiteit in Nederland. Studie van een emancipatiebeweging.* Amsterdam: Boom Meppel.
Warning, R. (Ed.). (1975). *Rezeptionsästhetik.* Munich: W. Fink.

APPENDIX

Readers were given a list of 55 book titles and 18 film titles. These titles were selected with an eye to general availability, and (for book titles) with an eye to including as many different "types" of texts as possible, i.e., youth literature, novels, writing by gay and non-gay authors, "classics" of various genres, sex-information titles. With two exceptions, the 18 book titles and 12 film titles which were read by the most respondents were then used for analysis and interpretation.

For each title the following questions were asked: (a) had the respondent read the book/seen the film; (b) how old the respondent was at this point; and (c) what the respondent thought about the book/film in general the first time it was read/seen. For these, a scale was indicated: very good, good, so-so, bad, don't know.

Further, (d) what the respondent thought about the "image of homosexuality" the book/film presented the first time they read/saw it; for this question this scale was indicated: very positive, reasonably positive, mixed (negative/positive), negative, very negative, didn't know/no longer knew/gave no image of homosexuality at all.

Cluster analyses were performed on all titles for the categories of "general finding" and "image of homosexuality" to facilitate our interpretative work, prompting the question: (e) whether the book/film was used as an occasion to talk with others about homosexuality.

The First Years
of a Consultation Bureau
for Homosexuality

Riek Stienstra
A. X. van Naerssen
University of Utrecht

ABSTRACT. The COC's attempt to form a consultation bureau which would supply social aid to homosexuals is presented. The details and problems of forming such a group, including financial matters, type of aid to be supplied, and staffing, are discussed. In conclusion, the total reformation of the bureau in the 1980's is explained. The reformation reflects the change in social tolerance toward homosexuality in The Netherlands.

In 1964, the COC (Cultuur en Ontspanningscentrum, Cultural and Recreational Centre, the main Dutch organization of homosexuals, founded in 1946) attempted to create an organized form of social aid to homosexuals. Up to that point, the COC had organized weekly consultation hours staffed by volunteers who dealt chiefly with concrete problems connected with homosexuality, such as housing, work, and legal aid, rather than with psychological problems. The COC contacted the National Council for Social Work (NCWS), which called a meeting with representatives from institutions dealing with mental health, parole assistance (morals laws then in force made homosexual contacts with persons under 21 punishable by law), marital and sexual problems, and from the Federation of General Practitioners. In

Riek Stienstra is Managing Director of the Schorer Foundation. Correspondence may be addressed to the authors, Nieuwendijk 17, 1012 LZ Amsterdam, The Netherlands.

addition, a representative from the Ministry of Culture, Recreation and Social Work, a psychiatrist, and a member of the COC took part in the discussions. Within this group the views on homosexuality were quite diverse. In the light of the political situation of the time (see Tielman, this issue), one had to reckon with opinions on homosexuality prevalent in the most important confessional groups, groups within which moral aspects of homosexual behavior were central. Agencies for social work used, as either their explicit or implicit guideline, the psychiatric views of homosexuality as a neurosis. Besides this, a liberalizing trend had concurrently begun in The Netherlands, initiating a process which would lead to broad discussions on matters such as marriage and the family, pornography, and abortion.

Within the advisory group it appeared impossible to work out a unanimous position on homosexuality at short notice, and for this reason the NCSW proposed that discussion not be directed toward the fundamental question of how homosexuality should be judged morally and scientifically. The necessity of providing social aid in cases involving problems related to homosexuality was recognized by all participants in the advisory group, who addressed themselves to the question of whether such aid should be provided through existing channels or by a separate agency. The Dutch Society for Sexual Reform was alone in favoring the former option. The advisory group decided that a separate agency would be formed, with representatives from existing agencies and homosexual groups as board members. In addition, the composition of the Board was to reflect the most important confessional groupings in The Netherlands—Protestant, Roman-Catholic, Jewish, and Humanistic. In 1965, a commission set up according to these criteria began to work out concrete plans for a consultation bureau for homosexuals.

In this second phase, besides working out financial matters and finding premises, the commission focused on the issue of what type of social aid should be provided. It was assumed that the agency's work would involve dealing with relatively complex psychological problems. The strenuous requirements set by the Dutch Government for subsidies to new agencies for social work were met, for the complexity of the problems to be dealt with validated the existence of the agency. In setting down job requirements for the future staff, the commission determined that psychiatric expertise among the psychiatrists, psychiatric social workers, and clinical psychologists involved would be a primary criterion for taking an intra-psychic, as opposed to social, approach to problems related to homosexuality.

The commission decided that, in light of the diverging and sometimes controversial views on homosexuality within Dutch society, the consultation bureau should not involve itself in disseminating information on homosexuality to the general public.

Another topic of discussion was the bureau staff's personal experiences with homosexuality. The COC alone maintained that it would be useful if one of the staff members was homosexual, a position that was rejected by a majority of the commission for fear that the bureau would isolate itself within the broader field of social services, and that personal involvement with homosexual problem areas could have a detrimental effect on the consultation process. The commission expressed no preference as to what the gender of the bureau's employees should be, even though the general expectation was that the problems to be handled would be encountered chiefly among homosexual men.

On November 14, 1968, the Schorer Foundation (named for the founder of the Dutch Scientific Humanitarian Committee, Dr. J. A. Schorer), the consultation bureau for homosexuality, was opened by the State Secretary for Culture, Recreation, and Social Work. The staff consisted of a psychiatrist, a psychiatric social worker, two psychologists, and two social workers. The Foundation's resources soon proved to be insufficient, for there were 500 applicants in two years; 1-1/2 years later 194 of these were still on the waiting list. For a year following this no new clients were accepted. Due to the strong emphasis it placed on psychiatric help, the Foundation conducted lengthy and intensive intake procedures for each client, procedures which discouraged many potential clients from seeking the Foundation's assistance. As a result of the ensuing one-sided selection of clients with middle and high education levels, the make-up of the staff and treatment procedures were altered, and intake procedures were simplified whereby they were no longer conducted exclusively by the psychiatrist and the psychologists. Changes were undertaken amidst lively internal discussion, fed by the critical interest shown by outsiders. In a letter to the Foundation, the militant, emancipation-oriented Federation of Student Workgroups on Homosexuality noted their impression that the counseling offered there was exclusively of a psychiatric nature, and noted further that the Foundation's philosophy pertaining to homosexuality was unclear. The Federation believed that homosexuality was not fully accepted within the Foundation; the latter defended themselves against this criticism in public by issuing the following statement:

> The Schorer Foundation operates on the basis of a complete acceptance of the [homosexual]. By "acceptance" is meant:
>
> a. That [homosexuality] is seen as a form of the experience of sexuality which deserves as positive an evaluation as does heterosexuality, the basic principle underlying social aid being that it is right and justifiable to help the individual to accept and develop a homosexual orientation.
>
> b. That in principle no preference be given for a young person's developing in a heterosexual or [homosexual] direction, provided that he or she develops in the direction that most adequately corresponds to his or her capabilities.
>
> c. That the criterion for providing social aid rest solely in helping to clear up social and psychic barriers to further developing the emerging "disposition" or preferential tendency, whereby the possibility is kept open that behavioral patterns and needs will be developed which are totally dif-

ferent from the ones which are currently customary and socially acceptable.

With this one standpoint, the complete acceptance of homosexuality, the Foundation presented a unified front to the outside world, but internal differences were great, as we see from the following statements made by staff members.

The psychiatric social worker: "There's a difference between the group with social problems and the group of clients with intra- and inter-psychic conflicts. Among those we don't see at the bureau there's a very neurotic group. With regard to the specifics of the client-group: the majority of [homosexuals] are psychodynamically disturbed; perhaps there's a psychological basis for this."

The social worker: "The bureau's clients are [homosexuals] who are conscious of feelings of dissatisfaction and unease as the result of social and intra-psychic factors. Clients in general are neurotic, but are so relatively un-neurotic in the face of concrete social problems. The very neurotic don't show up at the bureau because they're too little motivated. [Homosexuality] is probably more neurotic to the extent that it is coupled with an aversion to heterosexual contact."

The psychiatrist: "The clients of this bureau are just about all neurotic and this is because they're homosexual, but they're less neurotic than the group we're not seeing. In general, neurosis occurs more often among homosexuals than among heterosexuals. Homosexuality is often connected to negative Oedipal ties. Clients who ask themselves "Am I homosexual?" are generally inhibited sexually, therefore it's a neurosis. They must be seen first by the psychiatrist, after which psychotherapy must be prescribed."

The social psychologist: "The neurotic client group, not necessarily homosexual, is characterized by feelings of dissatisfaction and unease and by feeling a discrepancy between what one is and what one might be. The clinical group is characterized by serious depressions, a tendency toward suicide, with a strongly active and psychopathic or psychotic aspect. The goal of treatment is the reduction of neurosis, an increase in self-respect—whether as a homosexual or not.''

In dealing with client problems related to homosexuality, the Foundation had primarily to consider whether the intra-psychic, and initially primarily psychoanalytic approach, should be used, or whether more attention should be paid to social factors such as discrimination against, and social prejudice toward, homosexuality.

The break-up of the staff was also precipitated by a second factor. Although when the Foundation was being set up organizers had decided not to hire homosexual staff members, in practice it appeared that a number were homosexual. In staff discussions, the Foundation never clarified what effect a social worker's sexual preference could have on his job performance. Instead, the Foundation restricted itself to reformulating the organization's general goals, determining its priorities, and introducing new working methods, without ever resolving the contradictory views on homosexuality underlying its work. The basic demand for a cohesive and systematic view of homosexuality remained unanswered; the opposition between social and intra-psychic models remained obscured.

In 1972 the board decided to dismiss the entire staff. From that moment the new staff gradually developed new methods for the counseling of homosexuals. (See the article by van Naerssen in this issue.) The situation in the mid-1980s is completely different. The Foundation has a special section for the development of prevention programs. The counseling section works with an approach that focuses on problems related to sexual orientation (for example, development of an adequate gay/lesbian lifestyle) and not on the homosexuality of the clients as an intra-psychic process only. Perhaps more important, the majority of the staff is openly homosexual, and so are the members of the Board. This situation reflects the process of change in social tolerance to homosexuality in The Netherlands. At the same time, integration of counseling of homosexual clients in the general consultation bureaus is still not possible, probably due to the different lifestyles of many homosexuals.

REFERENCES

The material for this article is almost completely based on the Archives of the Schorer Foundation. In these Archives (1964-1972) the words homophilia and homophile are used instead of homosexuality and homosexual. Address: Nieuwendijk 17, 1012 LZ, Amsterdam, The Netherlands.

Theories on Homosexuality
Among Professional Therapists

A. X. van Naerssen
University of Utrecht

ABSTRACT. Current viewpoints on homosexuality among Dutch psychiatrists and psychologists in the period of 1945 to 1980 are discussed. In a detailed examination of these differing theories, a change in the approach to therapy with homosexual clients unfolds, incorporating more of a sociodynamic focus as compared to the psychodynamic concepts of earlier theorists.

During the period 1967 to 1972, attempts to provide adequately organized counseling for homosexuals in The Netherlands were not successful (Stienstra & van Naerssen, this issue). An important cause for this was that there wasn't a cohesive policy on homosexuality at the consultation bureau for homosexuality (Schorer Foundation). Stienstra and van Naerssen further pointed to the contradictions between the views of psychiatrists and psychologists on the one side, and social workers on the other. Among the former, an intra-psychic approach to homosexuality was predominate, an approach in which social factors, particularly discrimination against homosexuality and the influence of such discrimination on the homosexual's self-acceptance and acquisition of a sexual indentity, remained unexplored.

This article shall describe more closely the various viewpoints on homosexuality that were current among Dutch psychiatrists and psychologists in the period of 1945 to 1980. While most therapists demonstrated a certain tolerance toward homosexuality and the majority of them rejected the illness model which would dictate change in homosexual orientation, as a profession they nevertheless failed to analyze social discrimination against homosexuals and the effects it had on their homosexual clients. On the one hand, it was stated that homosexuality was the same thing as heterosexuality: Beyond the matter of sexual preference, there were no essential differences. Yet at the same time, it was denied that in a society where homosexuality was discriminated against, the personal exploration and realization of homosexual desires in fact could lead to specific problems among homosexuals. In the practical work of providing counseling, this led to a dilemma, for during therapy, the neutrality of the therapist was called for; the therapist was not to choose for or against homosexuality. The client's problems, however, arose precisely in a situation which was anti-homosexual. Thus, for the therapist it was often impossible to remain neutral. As a result, therapists often chose one of a number of approaches with which to attempt to deal with this dilemma.

THE RELIGIOUS MORAL APPROACH

In 1948 the psychiatrist F. J. Tolsma wrote an influential book entitled *Homosexuality and Homoeroticism*, in which he attempted to develop a Protestant-Christian view of homosexuality. First, he argued that biological research had not proven that homosexuality was genetically determined. According to Tolsma, the psychological concepts of Freud and Adler, which described homosexuality as a preference acquired during early childhood, provided no basis for developing a comprehensive view of homosexuality; the existing scientific approaches were, in essence, materialistic. A person's life, however, was neither unconditionally bound to a defective constitution nor to a life-history characterized by trauma. Of transcending importance was human freedom. Homosexuals ultimately could choose how to express themselves sexually. But as Protestant morality recognized heterosexual marriage as the only valid norm, the homosexual's choice would have to be celibacy. Non-sexual friendships between members of the same sex were indeed possible, but the love expressed in such relationships would always be inferior to love between men and women.

Tolsma was scarcely concerned with therapy for homosexuals. He assumed implicitly that treatment of adults directed toward changing sexual preference was seldom successful. Therapy was to emphasize and uphold Christian ethics. Parents, in turn, needed to guard against the possible development of homosexuality behavior in their children: discourage effeminate behavior in boys and tomboyish behavior in girls; check homoerotically tinged games during the pre-puberal phase; encourage heterosexual interaction during puberty; prevent regular contacts between the young and homosexual teachers or other homosexual adults, Tolsma regretted that so much youthful homosexual behavior did not come to the attention of psychiatrists, and was of the opinion that hormone therapy might be appropriate for the young. His view that homosexuality could arise via seduction was shared by many of his colleagues, and was reflected in Dutch laws pertaining to homosexual contacts. (See Salden's article, this issue.)

In 1967 the psychologist A. van den Aardweg published his study, "Homophilia, Neurosis and Compulsive Self-Pity." In that analysis of homosexuality, he defined neurosis as a compulsive tendency toward self-pity. Such self-pity manifested itself in constant complaining and psychological and somatic feelings of dissatisfaction and unease, complaining which seemed unjustified when considering the patients' lives objectively. According to van den Aardweg, the homosexual was characterized by such compulsive self-pitying, the origin of which lay in early childhood. The young child could become involved in situations which were detrimental to self-image, and had a tendency strongly to dramatize these situations. The pre-homosexual boy saw himself as an outsider because compared to others, he showed less bravado, was more prone to tears, and was somehow less than "all boy." His great yearning was to be accepted by such peers; the longing for homosexual contacts was, therefore, a longing to be admired by those he wished to be like. A comparable mechanism predicated on feminine traits applied to the pre-homosexual girl. Therapy for the adult homosexual consisted of having him/her perceive the basis of self-pitying behavior, while insuring that the appropriate gender role be learned.

In a later study (1981), van den Aardeweg evoked "nature laws" and "an evolutionary model," writing:

> Take for example the lesbian woman: Anatomically and physiologically, all the functions are present in a refined state which are clearly geared to reproduction; only the last link of the chain, erotic feelings for the object (the male) that would realize the intended goals of such functions, is missing. If Nature had "decided" to produce a type of human being that felt sexual desire for members of the same sex, it would have proceeded in a more efficient way and would have dispensed with that totally superfluous biological sexual mechanism.

PSYCHOANALYSIS

Well-known psychiatrists such as van Emde Boas (1965) and Kuiper (1974), whose views were chiefly influential in the teaching of medicine, based their work on psychoanalysis. They maintained that certain events have taken place in the psychosexual history of homosexuals which block the development of heterosexual preference. The homosexual male has an intense fear of woman; the lesbian woman is afraid of men.

As was the case with the authors mentioned earlier, the therapy advocated by van Emde Boas and Kuiper was primarily directed toward helping clients gain insight into their disturbed gender-role behavior. Van Emde Boas's assumption was, moreover, that homosexual preference is unchangeable after puberty. Until 1981, Kuiper defended the thesis that homosexuality is a neurosis. At that time, he distanced himself from that view in a lecture entitled "Notes on Homosexuality from Psychoanalytic

Practice." He did so, however, while at the same time stating that many problems experienced by homosexuals have their roots in unresolved Oedipal conflicts.

None of the authors mentioned up to now described social views of homosexuality in their analyses. This is remarkable, in that around 1970 the findings of a number of large-scale research projects were published in which it was shown that social tolerance in The Netherlands toward homosexuality was limited. (See Straver, 1976.) Data for these studies were obtained from a representative sample of the Dutch population above the age of 21, as well as from representative samples of general practitioners, youth leaders, and teachers in educational institutions.

HOMOSEXUALITY AND SELF-ACCEPTANCE

The doctoral thesis of W. J. Sengers, *Homosexuality As a Complaint,* (1969) marked a turning point in the views of homosexuality sketched above. He began by showing that in the psychiatric literature some 120 cases had been reported of attempts to resolve homosexual preference into a heterosexual one. With a single exception, none of these attempts had succeeded. Sengers also ascertained that the diagnostic terminology used for homosexuality was unclear, among other reasons, because of the use of such terms as latent homosexuality, pseudo-homosexuality, and homoeroticism. He proposed differentiating between homosexual behavior and homosexual orientation. According to Sengers, an analysis of orientation is necessary in determining who is and who is not homosexual. A person is homosexual who feels attracted exclusively to persons of the same sex and who has mastubatory fantasies and reports dreams whose manifest content exclusively features the same sex. By 1975 this "triad" developed by Sengers appeared to have been adopted by many Dutch professors of psychiatry (Sengers, 1975).

As homosexuals differ from heterosexuals only in their sexual preference and, in Sengers' terminology, are "just the same as anybody else,'' and as change in this preference is not effected by therapy, Sengers proposed that therapy be geared toward self-acceptance. In principle all homosexuals can be placed into 1 of 3 categories according to their attitudes toward their own sexuality. These psychological categories are resistance, ambivalence, or acceptance. Sengers established these categories of psychological resistance to homosexuality on the basis of no fewer than 50 characteristics. A few characteristics of resistance are, for example: denying one's orientation to third persons, preoccupation with sex, infantile fears, not daring to take risks, poor judgmental abilities, need of reinforcement, conformity. He admitted that this list of variables is long and convoluted, but felt unable to indicate which of the above characteristics are important, and which are less important. Apart from this, Sengers believed that the factors leading to a person's non-acceptance and resistance of his sexual orientation must be sought in the fact that the young homosexual discovers himself feeling things which are viewed by others as abnormal, deviant, sick, or sinful. With this opinion, Sengers became the first psychiatrist to introduce social factors as causes for intra-psychic conflicts. He did not, however, analyze the structure and the effect of such forms of discrimination. Therapy is geared to accepting one's feelings. In this process, according to Sengers, a strictly neutral position must be taken by the therapist; he is not permitted to advise a patient to look for, or to avoid, homosexual or heterosexual contacts. So Sengers didn't solve the therapeutic dilemma. The therapist had to be neutral although the social factors that led to homosexuality as a complaint were working against being homosexual.

THE NEUTRALITY OF THERAPISTS

Sengers's views were quite influential among both professionals and laymen. Various research projects on the development of a homosexual identity (Moerings & Straver, 1970, Sanders, 1977) emphasized the value which must be attached to accepting homosexual feelings. Sanders demonstrated that a positive attitude toward the homosexual on the part of parents and friends was of great influence in this process, a phenomenon which opened discussion on Sengers's thesis that a neutral attitude on the part of the therapist positively influenced the process of self-acceptance. By taking a positive attitude, one encouraged a person to give expression to homosexual longings, which one regarded as of the same value as heterosexual longings. It was precisely in surroundings where homosexual feelings were accepted as legitimate that resistance and ambivalence did not seem to appear. Among professionals, however, as publications of the staff of the Schorer Foundation showed, the neutral role of of the therapist was soon considered the norm, not the exception.

De Regt and Van Stolk (1979) set forth how problems related to self-acceptance were handled in professional practice. Their analysis centered on 3 factors: guilt feelings, damaged ideal self-image, and the fear of stigmatization. As far as it could be determined, guilt feelings were an issue chiefly among people with a strict religious upbringing. Fear of stigmatization referred back to social influences on homosexuality; fear of rejection, denigrating remarks, negative value judgments, and forms of discrimination were at the heart of such influences. And a damaged ideal self-image, according to these authors, lay at the core of problems with self-acceptance. Being homosexual could disrupt the experience of what and who one is or imagines oneself to be, and such a disruption could, in turn, be a source of potential trauma.

Regensburg, Citroen, and Van Stolk (1981) followed these views and pointed out again that in treating problems related to self-acceptance, the therapist must not chose for or against homosexuality. When treating such problems, partiality on the part of the therapist could be disastrous. They wrote:

At a consultation bureau for homosexuals it is probable that people with very serious problems with self-acceptance can't be helped: The professional who has anything to do with homosexuality is as threatening (and appealing) as homosexuality itself; the value-judgment of the professional who has anything to do with homosexuality is as objectionable as homosexuality itself.

Although Sengers proposed that the homosexual or heterosexual preference of a therapist made no difference as long as the therapist experienced sexuality in an integrated way, in the practical application of his theory the open homosexuality of the therapist or, as the case may be, the open support of homosexual longings was rejected. In the years to follow, this contradiction continued to dominate the discussion of professional counseling for homosexuals. Was the therapist to take sides? and if so, in what way?

THE OFFICIAL STANDPOINT OF THE PSYCHOLOGISTS AND THE ALTERNATIVES

In 1981-1982, an intense debate took place within the Dutch Federation of Psychologists on the issue of homosexuality as a neurosis, and on the moral aspects of the therapies geared to change sexual orientation. The Federation's Board ended the discussion by issuing three statements stating that : (1) A moral judgment of a homosexual orientation as bad or deviant was rejected; (2) An axiomatic connection between homosexuality and neurosis had not been proven; and, (3) Assistance could not be denied those wishing a change in sexual orientation; the effect of treatment geared to change this had not yet been sufficiently researched. What the Board chose not to do, however, was to acknowledge or comment at all on therapies geared toward the acceptance of homosexuality.

As a consequence of the statements the debate on adequate

counseling of problems around the development of a homosexual identity was held outside the Federation. At this moment there are at least three important points of view.

1. Pheterson (1979, 1982) focuses on the psychological internalization of social oppression. She recognizes the same system in black, Jewish and lesbian women and proposes the formation of social alliance groups. In these groups discussions are held between women on the differences and similarities of their oppression and their effects on social and individual functioning.

2. Van Naerssen (1986) makes a distinction between identity problems and relational problems. In the development of a sexual identity a person is primarily concentrated on the definition of the self as an autonomic entity. A person strives to a situation in which there is optimal self-esteem. A lot of expectations, fears and irrational attitudes are frustrating this process. Problems are mainly due to traumas in the personal history, so the counseling is focused on the processes of concept formation, especially the concepts of sexuality and homosexuality in relation to love and intimacy.

In relational problems the focus is on the interaction between two persons of the same sex. For these problems group psychotherapy is more adequate, so gay men and lesbian women can communicate on the difficulties they have in initiating and sustaining a relationship. As long as there is no social model for homosexuals (as the marriage is for heterosexuals), gays and lesbians can learn from each other how to handle relational problems around power, dependency, autonomy and love.

3. Schippers & Van Werkhoven (1984) makes the same distinction as Van Naerssen, but they put more weight on homosexual lifestyles, the social arrangements between man and between women.

So the differences between living alone, living in a closed or an open couple get more attention in their counseling. The general trend among professional therapists is to see homosexuality no longer as a psychological phenomenon and using psychody-

namic concepts to explain it. Instead there seems to grow a con-
senus to an interactionistic approach giving more attention to
sociodynamic factors in homosexual relations.

REFERENCES

Aardweg, G. J. A. van den (1967). *Homofilie, neurose en dwangzelfbeklag.* Amster-
dam: Polak en van Gennep.
Aardweg, G. J. A. van den (1981). *Homofiele pressie op het NIP de Psycholoog.*
Emde Boas, C. van (1965). Enkele aspecten van het probleem van de mannelijke
homosexualiteit. *Huisarts en Wetenschap.*
Kuiper, P. C. (1974). *Neurosenleer.* Deventer.
Kuiper, P. C. (1981). *Werkschets over homosexualiteit.* Amsterdam.
Moerings, M., & Straver, C. J. (1977). *Homofiele jongeren in relatie tot hun omgev-
ing.* Zeist.
Naerssen, A. X. van (In press). *Relaties tussen therapie en subkultuur bij de hulp aan
sexuele problemen.*
Pheterson, G. (1979). *Liberation with alliance: A draft proposal for work group of
black, Jewish, lesbian and allied women for experimental and theoretical similar-
ities and differences of oppression.* Amsterdam: Ivabo.
Pheterson, G. (1982). Bondgenootschap tussen vrouwen. Een theoretische en em-
pirische analyse van onderdrukking en bevrijding. *Psychologie en Maatschappij.*
Regensburg, R., Citroen, P., & Stolk, B. van (1981). Homosexualiteit, acceptatie en
behandeling. *Maanblad Geestelijke Volksgezondheid.*
Regt, J., & Stolk, B. van (1979). Zelfaanvaarding van homosexuelen. *Maanblad
Geestelijke Volksgezondheid.*
Sanders, G. (1977). *Het gewone en het bijzondere van de homosexuele leefsituatie.*
Deventer.
Schippers, J., & Werkhoven M. van (1984). Homosexualiteit en hulpverlening.
Handboek seksuele hulpverlening.
Sengers, W. J. (1969). *Homoseksualiteit als klacht. Een psychiatrische studie.*
Bussum: Paul Brand.
Sengers, W. J. (1975). *Antwoorden van hoogleraren psychiatrie op zeven vragen over
homoseksualitiet.* Rotterdam: Erasmus University Press.
Straver, C. J . (1976). Research on homosexuality in The Netherlands. *The
Netherlands Journal of Sociology, 12,* 121-137.
Tolsma, F. J. (1948). *Homosexualiteit en homoerotiek.* Daamen: S' Gravenhage.

The Dutch Penal Law
and Homosexual Conduct

Maarten Salden
University of Amsterdam

ABSTRACT. The history of changes in Dutch penal law regulating homosexual conduct since the 18th century are traced and their effects on homosexual behavior described. Changes in policies and practices regarding enforcement are reviewed. The article discusses the Dutch criminal code of 1886, the criminalization of homosexual contacts involving minors in 1911, the criminalization of male homosexuality from 1941 to 1945, and the progressive relaxation of the law since World War II, resulting in the decriminalization in 1971 of homosexual contacts involving minors and the draft in 1981 for a bill that would prohibit discrimination against homosexuals.

MAJOR DEVELOPMENTS

According to Dutch penal law, homosexual behavior as such has not been a crime since 1811, the year the French Penal Code became operative in The Netherlands. The Dutch Penal Code, which dates back from 1886, maintained this impunity. But it introduced an age-limit: Sexual intercourse by an adult with a minor below the age of 16 became punishable irrespective of the sex of the partners. In 1911 the Penal Code was extended with Article 248bis, which criminalized, with a maximum prison term of 4 years, any adult who had sexual intercourse with a partner of the same sex below the age of 21. In 1941, during the

---

Mr. Salden works in the Criminology Department of the University of Amsterdam, and is currently preparing a dissertation on the historical developments in the Dutch penal law regarding homosexual behavior. Correspondence may be addressed to the author, Criminologisch Instituut "Bonger," Kloveniersburgwal 72, Postbus, 19090, 1000 GB Amsterdam, The Netherlands.

155

German occupation an ordinance was issued forbidding sexual contacts between men of any age. In 1945, when the Germans had left the country, this ordinance was repealed. Article 248bis was abolished in 1971. In recent years a bill has been in preparation which would prohibit discrimination on the ground of sexual preference. This article is an outline of some of the political and social developments that influenced these alterations in the Dutch penal law.

FROM CAPITAL PUNISHMENT TO IMPUNITY

Compared to its neighbor nations, in the 1700s the Government of the Republic of The United Netherlands distinguished itself by exhibiting a great deal of political and religious tolerance. In the provincial and local corporations the citizenry formed the major political party, not the nobility or the clergy. In spite of Calvinism being the state religion, the clergymen did not decide the policy of the authorities. However, in the 18th Century the reigning individuals and families increasingly formed a close caste of regents, and the Republic gradually developed into a moderate monarchical form of government, especially after William IV of the House of Orange became the hereditary Stadtholder in all the provinces in 1747. Yet the Patriotic Party's resistance against this development grew.

The Republic was a confederation of states with no central legislature. Cities, villages, and polders were free to make their own laws. The highest legal authority was with the separate provinces. Unlike the system of the Middle Ages, local laws did not automatically break provincial laws. The provincial Courts of Justice exercised supervision over the lower government organizations. In addition, jurisdiction was not only based on chosen regulations but also on customs, Roman and Mosaic law, and the works of juridical authors.

Several local and provincial regulations ordained capital punishment for the "sin against nature" or the ignominy men commit with men, or women with women. Basing their verdict on custom and Roman and Mosaic laws, authoritative jurists concluded that "sodomites" should die on the stake. Otherwise, God would punish the whole community the way He had punished Sodom.

However, the risk of discovery of this behavior was small as long as it did not take place out in the open and no third party was involved. The difficulty of finding evidence, and the gravity of the crime, led the legal authorities to torture suspects severely. This often resulted in confessions and information about others, and in turn may partially account for the phenomenon that, after a long absence of trials against sodomites a single, accidental arrest might lead to a whole series of criminal cases. That was, for example, what happened with the wave of persecutions around 1730. Various locations in the Republic turned out to be meeting places for men who were looking for sexual contacts with other men. During this persecution, the question arose as to how to handle these cases legally. What, for instance, was to happen to those individuals who could not be charged with sodomy, but who had afforded the opportunity for others to participate in that activity? And what was to be done about those who, by escaping their towns, had managed to avoid prosecution by the municiple law court? Moreover, some lawyers appeared to have doubts as to the current explanation of the story of Sodom. (Anyone reading that biblical story will discover that there is no discussion of homosexual conduct as such, but of the rape of foreigners who were supposed to enjoy the right of hospitality.) In Amsterdam the flight of many well-to-do citizens caused a stir among the population. In an English journal the rumor was spread that certain wealthy citizens who had not yet succeeded in fleeing had been tried in secret, whereas the bodies of the average citizens were dangling from public gallows. In the province of Holland, the government issued a proclamation providing for public execution of individuals convicted of both sodomy and seduction to it. In addition, the government laid down the competence of the municipal law courts and the provincial courts of justice as to the prosecution of escaped suspects. Around 1764 sodomites in Amsterdam were publicly discovered gathering at various spots, e.g., public conveniences, although this appeared to have already been going on for quite some time. The government cited the Proclamation of 1730, and some lawyers argued that a conviction on the account of sodomy should require less evidence than other offenses. Yet Schomaker, a jurist who had been consulted, resisted this firmly.

While up until then complaints had mainly concerned the inconsistency and inequality of the existing laws, in the final quarter of the 18th Century some legal writers opposed the application of capital punishment and use of the rack in sodomy cases. To this end they referred to Montesquieu, Beccaria, and Voltaire. These philosophers of the Enlightenment reasoned that laws should not maintain a certain divine or traditional order, but guarantee the equality and freedom of the citizens, and pleaded that the people have a greater voice in government. They hoped to warrant equality by laying down civil rights in generally operative and unequivocal laws. In their view the best safeguard for freedom was a separation between law and morals, Church and State, crime and sin. Sodomy they considered a moral evil that could be fought by a sound upbringing, but they did not look upon it as a crime. The authorities should only punish what is demonstrably damaging to somebody else or the community. They were, moreover, strongly opposed to the cruel elements of penal laws that were in force at the time; namely, the use of torture and capital and corporal punishment. The well-to-do citizens of France, who had no political rights, especially favored these ideas. This was often attended by apostasy and anti-clericalism. The "National Assembly," summoned by the

French king in the winter of 1788-1789 (the first time since 1614), abolished the privileges of the nobility and clergy and issued the "Declaration of the Rights of Human Beings and Citizens." By ratifying a new penal law in 1791, the Assembly abolished corporal punishment and abolished punishment in cases involving homosexual contacts, as well as those involving heresy, sorcery, blasphemy, and witchcraft.

While in France citizens had to wrest political power from the nobility, clergy, and royal absolutism, the battle in the Republic of The United Netherlands was fought between the politically powerless citizens and the ruling bourgeois of regents. The libertine morals of the latter were frequently opposed to the "christian virtues" and "civil household" of the former. Here, too, radical views were held by those opposing the ruling factions, but the French "atheism" was generally condemned. As to homosexual contacts, some pleaded for the abolition of capital punishment, yet remained in favor of a long imprisonment. At first the patriotic tendency toward more political influence for the people was met with unwillingness on the part of the regents and adherents of the House of Orange.

With the advancement of the French army in 1795, the Patriots took power in The Netherlands. They set forth a Proclamation for The Netherlands which said that "Every human being has the right to serve God the way he either or not prefers without being forced in any way to do so." When, however, a jewish Dutchman concluded that this meant the abolition of all laws based on divine rights, a jurist named Gales answered that juridical research had borne out that the Proclamation of 1730 had not been rendered inoperative. Parliamentary elections excluded women as well as paupers and adherents of the House of Orange. The most important objective of the National Assembly, the drafting of a constitution, failed to be realized. No agreement could be reached on the issue of whether the new nation should be centrally governed or whether its provinces should be allowed great independence. The separation between Church and

State was another controversial issue. In The Netherlands this would amount to the cessation of calvinism as the State religion. The champions of such a separation found the catholics, who until then had been discriminated against, on their side. Problems arose as to what was to be done about the calvinist clergymen, who enjoyed state stipends, and the church buildings. And should schools henceforth be indifferent toward religion? A large number of representatives considered religion to be "the only source of salvation, good morals, and, inherent in that, happiness in the people."

The French broke through the irresolution by covering a coup d'état of advocates of a unitary state. The opponents of centralization were excluded from the new elections and this time a constitution was successfully drafted, one which proclaimed that "every citizen enjoys the freedom to serve God according to his heart's conviction" and that the Batavian Republic was one and indivisible. The highest authority was with the Representing Body, who chose a "Directoire" of 5 people to exercise the executive power. In addition, a general legal code was to be designed dealing with both civil and criminal laws, a process which ended up taking years. Meanwhile, justice was administered according to pre-1795 laws. People were still condemned for sodomy, and usually sentenced to hard labor. In the final decade of the 18th Century women were also among the convicts. In the meantime, Napoleon had risen to power to France. He welcomed the coup that took place in the Batavian Republic in 1801 led by a few members of the Directoire, who dissolved the Representing Body. The new constitution transferred legislative powers to the executive branch and restricted suffrage to well-to-do subjects. Both these institutions were to remain operative until late in the 19th Century. The new government set up a committee for framing a criminal code; the outcome of this included the proposal that "all sorts of acts of fornication, of what nature whatsoever, committed by men with men [women were not included here] or humans with animals," be punished with solitary confinement and life-long banishment, a punishment also applicable for those who made their houses available for the purpose. Those who encouraged others to commit this crime either by seduction or force were threatened with the rope. However, this bill was never passed. In 1805 Napoleon dissolved the government and appointed a Grand Pensionary. Under his reign an education act was ratified in which Christian virtues were laid down as the object of education.

In 1806 Napoleon, who meanwhile had been crowned emperor, turned the Batavian Republic into the Kingdom of The Netherlands. His brother Louis Napoleon, who was to lead the country, charged a committee with the framing of a criminal code. They proposed that "those guilty of committing fornication contrary to nature, with human beings [here women are included indeed] or animals, will be punished with long term imprisonment separated from all others, and life-long banishment from the realm." The same would await the one who made his or her house available for such activities. Those that dragged others into this crime, or put them up to it by force, abuse of authority, or excessive seduction, were, depending on the circumstances, threatened with either the rope, flogging, branding, long-term solitary confinement, or life-long banishment from the country. This bill was passed. The Criminal code for the Kingdom of The Netherlands became operative on February 1, 1809. Yet it was to be operative for only 2 years. After Napoleon declared The Netherlands a province of France, from March 1, 1809 forward the French criminal code, The Code Penal which had come into force under Napoleon, was applicable here. This law observed stricter penalties and recognized more offenses than the aforesaid French penal code from 1791. However, neither the French State Council nor the courts of justice and the law courts which had all been consulted about the subject had deemed homosexual contacts punishable. The moral reprehensibleness of the phenomenon was not considered, in itself, to be sufficient reason for treating it as a crime.

In The Netherlands the Code Penal's underlying principle that justice and morals should be kept separate by no means found general support with regard to homosexuality. After Napoleon's defeat at Leipzig, a Dutch popular movement rose against the French, and some prominent citizens requested that Prince William of Orange become king of The Netherlands. A constitution was framed by a committee declaring that the legislative power was with the king and the States General and that a general code of Criminal Law was to be drafted. The king decided that for the time being the Code Penal should be used. He appointed a few hundred notable citizens who approved of the constitution. In 1815 they offered the king a draft of the Criminal Code for the Kingdom of The Netherlands. It was a revised version of the former criminal code, but it ordained the same heavy penalization of "unnatural fornication contrary to nature with human beings."

The great powers that gathered in Vienna after Napoleon's downfall in order to re-organize Europe wanted a strong nation bordering on the north of France. They decided to join Belgium and The Netherlands. With strong emphasis they stipulated that these countries had equal rights, a move which could only be effectuated by revising the Dutch Constitution (1815). Thus the Two Chambers system was introduced. The First was to be appointed by the king, the Second would be equally divided over The Netherlands and Belgium and consist of representatives who had been chosen through elections by indirect vote. Voting rights were reserved to a limited number of noblemen and prominent citizens. The Belgians did not care much for the Dutch bills. They preferred the French code, which they had been accustomed to for years. Thus, in the end, the Code Penal remained operative in The Netherlands, and consequently the impunity of homosexuality, a fruit of the Enlightenment and French Revolution was for The Netherlands the unintended result of those international political developments.

THE DUTCH CRIMINAL CODE (1886)
MAINTAINED THE IMPUNITY

The Code Penal ordained that no act was punishable unless a law applicable to it already existed prior to the commission of the act. Because the Code did not include a provision against homosexual conduct, such conduct was only punishable if it was covered by one of the other articles of the Code Penal. The Code Penal was very reserved regarding sexuality. Only rape, public violation of virtues, and pimping were threatened with punishment. In The Netherlands this code remained in force until 1886.

At first the majority of the members of the Dutch Parliament were conservative. A draft for the Dutch Criminal Code from 1827, which was never passed, contained the same heavy penalization for homosexual acts as was ordained by the Criminal Code of the Kingdom of The Netherlands (1809-1811). It was not until after the separation from Belgium that liberal ideas penetrated Dutch politics. With the protestants, liberalism manifested itself in the "Groningen School," which no longer looked upon the Old Testament as infallible. The catholics, who after the separation from Belgium had become a discriminated minority, placed their hopes on the liberal ideal of freedom, which started from the principle of a separation between Church and State. According to King William I's own words, the signs of revolution all over Europe in 1848 turned him overnight from a conservative into a liberal. He took the initiative in amending the constitution. The executive power was in the hands of the ministers, who were politically accountable to the representatives (Second Chamber). The franchise was conferred to those who paid a minimum amount of indirect tax. The majority of these distinguished middle-class men were liberal. In 1857 a new education act came into force that provided strict neutrality of State schools with regard to religion. Private education was allowed, but would not be granted State subsidy.

People holding different views started to assert themselves as well. Orthodox protestants repudiated the purely secular state, especially its favoring of State schools. The leader of these "anti-revolutionaries" was Abraham Kuyper. Opposing himself against the modernistic professors and theologians at the neutral universities he founded his own calvinist university in 1879, the Free University of Amsterdam. The catholics, too, turned away from liberalism. In 1864 the pope had repudiated many of the institutions of liberalism, socialism, communism, modern theology, and scriptural knowledge. In 1868 the Dutch bishops demanded education on religious principles. The catholics and protestants decided eventually to cooperate politically. As one of its goals, this christian coalition hoped to increase the number of its adherents by extending suffrage.

In The Netherlands the transformation from an agricultural into an industrial economy started rather late, not until the second half of the 19th Century. The industrial and agricultural laborers lived under very poor conditions, such as low wages, no social provisions, no political rights, bad housing, malnutrition, and the necessity for women and children to work. Some citizens became concerned for the physical, intellectual, and moral state of the laborers. A government committee appointed in 1869 to investigate these conditions revealed horrible facts. In the Regout glass-works in Maastricht small children worked day and night shifts. The death rate of these children between the ages of 7 and 12 was 4 times as high as that of middle-class children the same age. The average glass-cutter did not live beyond 30. The committee did not, however, recommend any measures be taken; according to the classically liberal theory, the state was not allowed to interfere in the competition between equal individuals.

Some liberals began to see the need for social legislation and extension of suffrage. The laborers had organized themselves, creating tension in industrial circles. Liberal gentlemen who feared the influence of the Marxist International founded the

General Dutch Workers League (ANMV), the first federation of unions, in 1871. Representatives of the middle class formed a "committee for the discussion of the social problem," and chose for partners in the talks the leaders of the labor movement and the liberal member of the Second Chamber, van Houten. They succeeded in bringing about the abolition of child labor due in part to support from the labor movement, who drew up a petition and staged a nationwide demonstration regarding this issue. A thoroughly modified version of the bill passed the Chamber, but no provisions were made for checking the observation of it. Nonetheless, the principle of non-interference had been abandoned.

In the labor movement a division came about. The campaign for better state schools that was conducted by the ANWV led the protestants to create The Christian Labor Union, and the liberal character of the ANWV made the marxist laborers decide to form a Socialist Union. Thus, Dutch society was split into three factions representing three concepts regarding the responsibility of the State, i.e., liberal, christian, and socialist.

Yet in parliament the majority still held liberal views. The bill of a committee that had been appointed by government in 1870 finally lead to an authentically Dutch criminal code. Passed in 1880 and effective from 1886, it was much stricter in the field of sexuality than the Code Penal. The penalties were more severe and more deeds were considered punishable. Sexual contacts with young people below the age of 16 would henceforth be punishable, even if there was no question of violence or public violation of virtues, and even if the younger party had taken the initiative. It also threatened to punish sexual contacts that had been brought about by abuse of authority over dependent persons, e.g., parents, guardians, and teachers toward minors and governors, and warders and medical doctors toward people of any age in asylums, prisons, and hospitals. Moreover, minors were henceforth forbidden to be in brothels. In all these cases, the State could institute legal proceedings irrespective of the sexual act being homosexual or heterosexual. Homosexuality, though, in itself was not punishable. The majority of the committee and of the Second Chamber held the liberal view that moral reprehensibleness alone was no reason for penalization by order of the government. A probably christian minority wished to penalize "unnatural fornication" because the public conscience considered it a crime, and because impunity would either run counter to respect for the law, or else diminish the gravity of the offense in the eyes of the people. The majority, however, rejected this, although they did not deny that it occurred every day and that it was a serious moral evil.

CRIMINALIZATION OF THE ADULT WHO "COMMITS FORNICATION" WITH A PERSON OF THE SAME SEX BELOW THE AGE OF 21 (1911)

Around the turn of the century new attempts were made to extend the public morality code. The extensions of suffrage in 1887 and 1896 involved middle-class and working-class men, which amounted to an increase of support for the christian parties in particular. The Social Democratic Labor Party, who wished to improve the workers' position through a democratic process, also grew in number and gained more and more seats in Parliament. An 1887 parliamentary inquiry into the degree in which the child labor law of van Houten was observed had brought to light astonishing facts, especially about the Regout factories in Maastricht, which deeply shocked the middle class.

It was not until 1890 that industrialization really started to develop. Hoping for better employment and living conditions in the industrial areas, many country dwellers moved to the cities. Here the enormous accumulation of people in bad accommodations laid a curse on large families and prompted the formation of a movement which advocated birth control, the New Malthusians. Among its members were many liberals. Socialists, too, supported the sale of contraceptives. Social views on sexuality and the relations between men and women changed, as did those regarding homosexuality. Discussing homosexuality ceased to be a taboo. The neurologist Von Romer set up an inquiry among students in Amsterdam. Of them 2.3 percent considered themselves avowed homosexuals. Schorer, a jurist, and Aletrino, a crimino-anthropologist, fought against prejudices and misconceptions. There were close contacts with the Wissenschaftlich-Humanitares Komitee in Germany, which in particular fought in their country the penalization of homosexual contacts between men.

From the turn of the century the christian parties were in control. They based their administrations on "christian principles." When Prime Minister Abraham Kuyper was asked for an explanation of his doctrine, he cited a speech by Aletrino, teacher at the neutral University of Amsterdam. At an international congress the latter had pleaded equal rights for homosexuality and heterosexuality. Kuyper said, "Now we have come so far that these ideas are not only expressed in secret, but also in public, I should like to ask whether the honorable representative would not sympathize with my opinion, that it is finally about time to intervene." In 1904 Schorer wrote in the juridical magazine "Themis" that expressions of true love cannot be regarded as acts of fornication, and that to homosexuals the satisfaction of their needs is completely natural. A member of the First Chamber, Van den Biesen, thought this horrible and asked, "Is it in this case surprising that christian parties unite and say to one another, 'This goes too far; we have to set bounds to this as much as possible'?"

The lack of state aid for private schools had brought the confessional faction together. Kuyper practically equalized the position of the private-school teachers to that of their state-school colleagues. In discussions of other social problems the christian principles by no means warranted unanimity. The Bible did not provide regulations for securities and collective labor agreements. Since 1891 governments had been trying to frame improved labor legislation. When in 1907 the confessional cabinet of De Meester brought in a bill, some industrialists turned against this innovation. They had for their advocate Louis Regout, a member of the First Chamber and of the Regout family who owned the factories in Maastricht which were known for their exploitation of children. The christian parties did, though, manage to achieve unanimity in their "fight against immorality." In 1904 Minister Nelissen introduced a bill containing provisions against abortion, the propaganda of birth-control among minors, brothels, pornography, and gambling. It also included an article (248bis) against the seduction of minors by prostitutes and through gifts and promises. The bill had already passed the State Council, who advises the government before bills are introduced to Parliament. When the article was discussed in the Committee of Justice in the Second Chamber, a minority turned out to be in favor of penalization of any homosexual conduct. Others pointed out that this would be in defiance of the Legal Code and its underlying principle that the authorities would not start legal proceedings unless somebody else or the community had been impaired. Still others asked for a regulation against adults who committed fornication with minors. No agreement was reached. One of the members of the committee was Edmond Regout, a brother of the aforesaid Louis Regout, who then held the post of minister. For years he had been pressing the combat against immorality. Due to illness, Nelissen had to resign and was succeeded by E. Regout. The latter proposed to make Article 248bis operative in order to protect minors against the homosexual fornication of adults "because it is the adult voluptuary who preferably seeks his victims among adolescents who are insufficiently experienced to immediately see through his evil intentions." (The age limit for heterosexual contacts remained 16.) This unparliamentary procedure, inserting a completely new provision in someone else's bill without consulting the State Council, earned the article the name of "cuckoo's egg of Regout."

Regout advanced various arguments. According to him the evil grew in the big cities, where quite a few persons supposedly became homosexuals through seduction. And the propaganda increased "in which it is represented as if it did not concern here one of the most perverted, decisively unnatural sins, but a, if not to be approved of, at least not reprehensible variety of the natural sexual instincts, which was scientifically and socially defensible."

That homosexuality was brought on by seduction was, however, already a much contested notion. And that homosexual activity took place every day was already widely known when the Penal Code of 1886 came into force. Although Regout failed to support his other arguments with evidence, an additional factor turned the tide. Having inquired about the matter, various members of the First Chamber who at first had refused to make it a crime now held that penalization was necessary, "in particular since a literature has gradually been developing through which the authors would have one believe that homosexuality is scientifically defensible." Socialists and liberals repudiated the plan, but their resistance was of no avail. The majority of the representatives were christians who thought that legislature, in determining what was punishable, should use God's will as a standard. The appeal to the Holy Scriptures and the church doctrine made the minority lament that "such people were not amenable to reason."

Besides Parliament, it was above all the authoritative professor and chief editor of the "Weekblad van het Recht," David Simons, who turned against this provision. He thought the general protection provided for the young until the age of 16 was sufficient and pointed out the danger of blackmail. In his leaflet "Tweeerlei Maat" ("Double Standard"), Schorer demonstrated that the article was discriminating. His leaflet was distributed on a large scale and also sent to members of the two Chambers, though in vain. The increasing number of "heathens" that pleaded a more tolerant attitude toward homosexuals were the very group Regout and his followers turned their crusade against. As their remarks in parliament bore out, they intended to prohibit these different views. But this would be a violation of the freedom of science and opinion. Yet being a majority, they could intensify the still existing repugnance by a penal provision. Thus, they publicly confirmed that the ''christian spirit of the people'' should be the basis of government and not the ''modern outlooks of life.''

PENALIZATION OF HOMOSEXUAL CONTACTS BETWEEN MEN OF ANY AGE (1940-1945)

The introduction of Article 248bis prompted Schorer to found a Dutch department of the Scientific Humanitarian Committee (the NWHK). At first there were only a few prosecutions based on this article, for from the beginning its enforcement presented the authorities with problems. New views on criminal law put the emphasis on the offender and his rehabilitation. (Women have scarcely ever been prosecuted under this provision.) Many cases that became known to the police involved men that made contacts in the street with young male prostitutes. The latter had to testify against the ''offenders.'' Policemen complained about this and pointed out the danger of blackmail; in fact, probation officers pointed out that usually respectable people were involved (often family men of good repute) who never otherwise violated the law. The number of paroles granted was high. The psychiatrists and psychologists appointed to investigate the matter complained that those involved showed little desire to be cured and would not acknowledge the reprehensibleness of their conduct.

With the elections of 1913 the socialists had scored again, but they refused to participate in the government. In view of the outbreak of World War I, during which The Netherlands preserved its neutrality, the factions decided to sink their differences. This truce fostered the establishment of a general franchise and the complete equalization of State and private education. The elections of 1918 marked a victory for the christian coalition and a great gain for the socialists; from that time forward catholics and socialists were to be the largest parties. In the 1920s the christian coalition, which had lasted for almost half a century, broke up when a proposal to close the Dutch legation at the Vatican passed the Chamber. The disagreement between the factions prevented them from establishing a stable majority in the Chamber. Also, the stock market crash in the United States caused great economic distress in The Netherlands. As a result of these developments, many started to doubt the value of parliamentary democracy.

In the 1930s the political and cultural differences became aggravated. A national-socialist movement appeared on the scene in 1931. The christian politicians kept complaining about the "demoralization" and loose views evident in advertisements, fashion, films, dance, and literature. Religious and national socialist movements emphasized the importance of a community based on nationalism and family life, and resisted the institutions that severed the link between sexuality and procreation. The New Malthusian Alliance and the NWHK were particularly affected by this conservative thinking. Although those who favored equal rights for homosexuals gradually grew in number, support from the socialist and liberal politicians, which they had enjoyed at the turn of the century, was quickly decreasing.

There were a few homosexual bars in the big cities, but they were permeated with a feeling of isolation. Voices were heard suggesting that the testicles of staunch offenders against the morality be removed, or that such offenders at least be sterilized, a punishment sometimes enacted against offenders of Article 248bis as a part of their medical "treatment." Psychological complications probably prevented the application of such treatment on a large scale. In 1938 the criminologist Feber observed that transgressions of Article 248bis occurred frequently for the very reason that a great many people did not have a moral objection to such behavior, and therefore it seldom came to the knowledge of the police. Yet Feber considered punishment necessary. Apart from the existing ground for penalization, namely that harm was done to somebody, the community would now add a new reason: deviation from collective values.

The first to offer homosexuals the opportunity of speaking extensively was Benno Stokvis in his book *De Homosexuelen, 35 Autobiographieen*. In reaction to it, Professor Van Bemmelen argued in *Het Nederlandse Juristenblad* (1939), a lawyers' magazine, that homosexuals were foreigners in state and society and, consequently, could not demand rights. Shortly before the outbreak of World War II, a few homosexuals published a magazine called "Levensrecht" ("The Right to Live").

A few months after the German invasion of The Netherlands, the state commissioner who had been appointed by Hitler proclaimed an ordinance for "the repression of unnatural fornication," whereby sexual contacts between men of any age became punishable. The members of the NWHK had to go underground, as did the editors of "Levensrecht." In its preface to a report on a congress about homosexuality organized in 1939, the Roman-Catholic Union of Physicians made clear in 1941 that there was no place for NWHK in the New Order of The Netherlands. A few raids on homosexual bars subsequently took place, but this never developed into systematic persecution. With the post-war liberation this ordinance was repealed.

THE ABOLITION OF ARTICLE 248bis

After the war the authors of "Levensrecht" re-emerged. Within this circle the Cultural and Scientific Recreation Center (COC) was established. This organization mainly focused on providing information and support to, and on creating meeting places for, homosexuals. In view of Article 248bis, minors were not admitted.

After the war catholics and socialists were to form the core of all government cabinets until 1958, the "Roman-Red Coalition." Early on the christian parties continued to complain about demoralization. Even as late as 1950 The Catholic Centre for Political Education proposed the penalization of all forms of homosexuality. The sexologist Van Emde Boas opposed this and went so far as to demand that Article 248bis be abolished. He expressed his ideas in the magazine of the Nederlandse Vereniging voor Sexuele Hervorming (the Dutch Society for Sexual Reform, the NVSH), the successor of the New-Malthusian alliance. However, the NVSH did not yet enjoy wide support.

But soon the tide began to turn. The coalitions of catholics and socialists laid the foundation for a welfare state, the number of soundly trained professional social workers was on the increase, and new scientific insights, which often were not that new at all as they had already been expressed at the turn of the century, took form in wider circles. The American Kinsey Report of 1948, in particular, undermined many prejudices. All sorts of (homo)sexual conduct turned out to be more widespread among minors and less harmful than had often been assumed. Those whose daily work involved interviews with homosexuals—psychologists, pedagogues, physicians, priests, and criminal law functionaries—started to wonder whether the taboo did not cause more damage than its actual transgression.

Furthermore, progressive ideas were developing in catholic and protestant circles. The catholic theology, in particular, acquired an international reputation. Around 1960 the post-war birth wave intensified the need for solutions to the problems created by overpopulation, and for a moral justification of the use of contraceptives. Sexuality was no longer looked upon as a mechanism necessary for procreation, but as an important medium for making contacts and forming relationships. Thus, homosexuality came up for discussion. In a number of articles in 1959 the protestant theologist Ridderbos rejected the traditional, biblical denunciation of homosexuality. The catholic organization of people who worked with the mental-health service chose homosexuality for their annual study day's subject in 1960, during which a plea was made for a form of assistance that supported rather than destroyed homosexual relationships. The catholic psychiatrist Trimbos gave a series of radio talks, four of which were on homosexuality. They drew a large audience. He argued that prejudices against homosexuals—for example, that they were effeminate, sex-maniacs, sick, and violators of boys—were scientifically untenable. And he stressed the resemblances between homosexual and heterosexual relationships. A group of scholars of the protestant Free University came up with similar ideas in the book *De Homosexuele Naaste,* as did the radio talks of pastor Kramer. A group of priests and pastors began to study the practical consequences for the spiritual guidance; this resulted in directives for catholic priests. The most important result of all this was the acceptance and support of homosexual relationships.

The freer ideas about sexuality found favor with wide strata of the society. The NVSH experienced unprecedented growth. COC's numbers grew as well, its members started to manifest themselves more openly, and in 1964 it set up "Dialoog," a foundation which homosexuals and heterosexuals operated jointly. In some big cities clubs were started for young homosexuals, clubs which admitted anyone, including heterosexuals. Several times the police threatened to take action against such clubs, but never followed through. And student workshops were formed, opening up additional possibilities for contacts between homosexuals. These developments all strengthened the self-respect of individual homosexuals and contributed to the possibility of "coming out."

Between 1958 and 1965 the christian and liberal parties were in power, a period followed by a temporary reinstatement of the Roman-Red Coalition. The return of the socialists brought a progressive government policy which sharply raised expenditures for all sorts of public and social provisions. In October of 1966 this cabinet fell on account of its budget policy. In 1967 it was succeeded by a catholic-protestant coalition. Under this government Article 248bis was abolished by parliament.

The public authorities, too, were influenced by the prevailing changes. The COC organized discussions between health-care institutions and the Minister of Social Affairs with a view to setting up consultation offices for homosexuals. In 1967 the first largely government subsidized office of the ''Jonkheer Schorer Stichting'' was opened in Amsterdam. The government also proceeded to finance a few extensive research projects. Criticism by the COC and the health-care profession against discrimination aimed at the homosexuals made application of Article 248bis an increasingly disputed issue. A growing number of specialists declared that it was impossible to turn somebody past the age of 16 into a homosexual through seduction.

Public prosecutors more and more decided against prosecuting cases coming under Article 248bis. The number of sentences for these offenses dropped from 181 in 1960 to 93 in 1966. Many representatives of the judiciary disagreed with the provision. Van der Waerden, a judge in Amsterdam, started a discussion of this issue in the scientific organ of the Socialist Labor Party; this is how the matter was eventually raised in Parliament.

In 1967 spokesmen of the liberals, socialists, and catholics pressed for the abolition of Article 248bis. They pointed out that the theory of seduction had been rendered out of date and that the article led to blackmail. The minister of justice promised an inquiry that was to be carried out by the undersecretary of social affairs and public health. The latter consulted the Health Council, whose task it is to inform the government about the scientific developments with respect to questions in the field of public health. The Council set up a committee which included among its members Trimbos and Van Emde Boas. This board heard representatives of the police, judiciary, the homosexual community, education and youth care, psychiatry, and social medical science. Many experts testified that the seduction theory had not been proved, that young homosexuals have need of identification with seniors, that the age limit of 21 hindered aid, that Article 248bis encouraged blackmail, and that other articles offered sufficient protection to minors. The committee unanimously concluded that there were no objectives of a medico-hygienic and psycho-social nature against the repeal of Article 248bis of the Criminal Code. On the contrary, they were convinced that a decriminalization had many advantages. The Minister moved the repeal. According to him, moral reprehensibleness was no reason for penalization. He also rejected the idea, which the committee had encountered, that the article should be maintained for some extreme cases. He argued that maintaining a penal provision not in order to apply it systematically, but only in some cases that are undefined in law, is incompatible with the demands of precision, definiteness, and protection against arbitrariness that can be made upon the Dutch Criminal Code and its application.

Nearly all parties in Parliament were in favor of abolishing the article. While finding a homosexual relationship less valuable than a heterosexual one, spokesmen of the large christian parties held that it was unjust to condemn someone who deviates from the normal pattern, and that the authorities, but for extreme cases, should not protect the field of intimate life via the criminal law. Without voting by call, the Second Chamber declared Article 248bis abrogated. Only three small right-wing parties, two of which were fundamentalist christian, requested that their negative votes be noted. In the First Chamber nobody wished to contest the abolition of the article. Here, too, in 1971, the article was declared abrogated without voting by call. Thus the "cuckoo's egg" of Regout was disposed of after 60 years. In that period more than 5000 people, mostly men, had been prosecuted and sentenced on the ground of this article.

INCREASING PROTECTION
AGAINST DISCRIMINATION

The abolition of Article 248bis passed the general population largely unnoticed. Among them prejudice and a lack of understanding still prevailed. In recent years, however, things seem to have been improving.

Having examined the public morality legislation, a later committee advised further decriminalization. They wanted to repeal the article against the seduction of minors by prostitutes and through gifts and promises, an article which has hardly ever been applied. They also proposed abolishing the penalization of sexual acts with persons in a dependent position (one's own children, stepchildren, foster children, staff members, pupils) above the age of 16. In addition, they wanted to add the clause that sexual contacts or similar conduct with children below the age of 16 be penalized only in cases where they had been forced to participate. Sexual intercourse or similar acts with children below the age of 12 should remain punishable. In other fields, especially indecent assault and rape and sexual relations between staff and patients in institutions, further criminalization was proposed.

A great many Dutch people, including religious people, have come to take more liberal attitudes toward homosexual and heterosexual conduct. Confronted with a sudden drop in the number of their representatives in Parliament in the late 1960s, the different christian parties agreed to join forces and founded the Christian Democratisch Appel. They succeeded to stay in power by forming coalitions with liberals or socialists. All of these political parties pay some degree of attention to the interests of women and homosexuals.

The conservative ideas, however, have not yet vanished. Some bishops, for instance, have firmly resisted the equalization of homosexuality and heterosexuality. Their views are supported by a statement of the Vatican Congregation for the Religious

Doctrine of 1976, and thus gave rise to discord within the college of bishops.

In the 1970s the strife for the equalization of men and women, homosexuality and heterosexuality, enjoyed wide support in the government and parliament. Support which in 1981 resulted in the draft for a bill prohibiting discrimination against persons on the ground of sex, sexual orientation, marital status, and living status (together or alone), in the areas of employment, education, trade and industry, or public authorities. However, led by the Evangelische Omroep (Evangelical Broadcasting Company), a few orthodox christian movements organized themselves against the plan. They met with much response on the part of the denominational schools and until the mid-1980's the bill had not been introduced. At this writing it cannot be foreseen how this will end. It ought to be borne in mind that only a minority of the Dutch population live according to the classical family pattern of father, mother, and children (in 1976—43%, in 1980—35%.) The majority live according to every conceivable variant: single, with mother, brother, friend, and so on. All these modes are placed at a disadvantage when compared with marriage. With an anti-discrimination bill, an attempt would be made to smooth away those differences in order to allow people to develop according to their own preferences.

In recent years, it has sometimes been possible to discuss discrimination based on sex and sexuality on an international level, which signifies an important breakthrough. When the United States decided not to allow homosexuals to enter their country, The Netherlands raised the matter before the Commission of Human Rights in the United Nations. In 1981 the Council of Europe repudiated the discrimination of homosexuals in a resolution that had been introduced by the Dutch socialist Voogd. A judgment by the Jurisdiction Department of the Dutch Council of State made The Netherlands the first country to acknowledge the principle that homosexuals who fear prosecution on account of their sexual inclination in their own country can ask for protection on the grounds of the Refugee Treaty of Geneva.

Nevertheless, in many countries there still exist laws and provisions directed against homosexual conduct. According to the Dutch delegation in the Commission of Human Rights, these regulations are as objectionable as measures that discriminate against race, religion, nationality, or philosophy.

Index